# Hov[illegible] Guide
# [illegible]g



## 101 Tips to Learn How to Serve, Give Excellent Customer Service, and Achieve Success as a Server in the Restaurant Industry

**HowExpert with Emma Eliason**



**www.HowExpert.com**

**For more tips related to this topic, visit HowExpert.com/serving**

# Recommended Resources

- HowExpert.com – Quick 'How To' Guides on All Topics from A to Z by Everyday Experts.
- HowExpert.com/free – Free HowExpert Email Newsletter.
- HowExpert.com/books – HowExpert Books
- HowExpert.com/courses – HowExpert Courses
- HowExpert.com/clothing – HowExpert Clothing
- HowExpert.com/membership – HowExpert Membership Site
- HowExpert.com/affiliates – HowExpert Affiliate Program
- HowExpert.com/jobs – HowExpert Jobs
- HowExpert.com/writers – Write About Your #1 Passion/Knowledge/Expertise & Become a HowExpert Author.
- HowExpert.com/resources – Additional HowExpert Recommended Resources
- YouTube.com/HowExpert – Subscribe to HowExpert YouTube.
- Instagram.com/HowExpert – Follow HowExpert on Instagram.
- Facebook.com/HowExpert – Follow HowExpert on Facebook.
- TikTok.com/@HowExpert – Follow HowExpert on TikTok.

# Publisher's Foreword

Dear HowExpert Reader,

HowExpert publishes quick 'how to' guides on all topics from A to Z by everyday experts.

At HowExpert, our mission is to discover, empower, and maximize everyday people's talents to ultimately make a positive impact in the world for all topics from A to Z...one everyday expert at a time!

All of our HowExpert guides are written by everyday people just like you and me, who have a passion, knowledge, and expertise for a specific topic.

We take great pride in selecting everyday experts who have a passion, real-life experience in a topic, and excellent writing skills to teach you about the topic you are also passionate about and eager to learn.

We hope you get a lot of value from our HowExpert guides, and it can make a positive impact on your life in some way. All of our readers, including you, help us continue living our mission of positively impacting the world for all spheres of influences from A to Z.

If you enjoyed one of our HowExpert guides, then please take a moment to send us your feedback from wherever you got this book.

Thank you, and we wish you all the best in all aspects of life.

Sincerely,

BJ Min
Founder & Publisher of HowExpert
HowExpert.com

PS...If you are also interested in becoming a HowExpert author, then please visit our website at HowExpert.com/writers. Thank you & again, all the best!

# Table of Contents

# Introduction

## I Swear I Know What I'm Talking About:

I was 18 years old when I was introduced to the service industry. I was a single teen mom, working a retail job, hardly making ends meet. I lived *barely* paycheck to paycheck, and as a result, I was incredibly stressed out. Not only did I have to pay for groceries with quarters and dimes, but I also had no extra money to spend on myself or my daughter.

I tried adding on more hours and more shifts, but in the end, I was missing valuable time with my baby and not even making a dent in my financial situation.

When my daughter was three months old, I decided something needed to change.

I can't remember who this guardian angel was, but if I could find them now, I would tell them their advice changed my life. Someone somewhere had suggested I try serving. According to them, waitresses made **very** good money, and "I had the outgoing personality for it." Of course, I was wary, I had never worked in a restaurant before, and I had no experience. But money was money, and I was willing to try anything at this point.

My very first serving job was at Buffalo Wild Wings. I started as a host but, after a year, made my way up to serving. The world of corporate restaurants was all I had ever known in the industry, so at the time, I had no idea I was capable of so much more.

Don't get me wrong; I am beyond thankful to have had Buffalo Wild Wings as my first serving job. I loved the atmosphere, I loved my coworkers, and I truly enjoyed my job. However, there were no standards or expectations on servers to be good at their jobs. They didn't care if you went above and beyond to make someone's experience memorable. They didn't care if you laughed with your table, cried with your table, or bonded with your table over something. They didn't care about how the servers performed; as long as the food was rung in right, drinks were full, and the customers had what they came for, you were golden.

I had a natural knack for serving. But I was a robot. I simply didn't understand that I could be personable with my customers. I didn't know I could ask questions about their lives. I didn't know I could be more than a waitress. I was just a number, just an employee.

That's the atmosphere in most corporate places. A corporate restaurant is where 90% of servers get their feet wet. This is because corporate chains will hire almost anyone, even those without previous serving experience. Because the bar is set so low for these servers, it essentially just provides a starting point for many of these waiters and waitresses to learn the very minimal, basic skills needed to be in the industry.

Flash forward a bit, and after a very heartbreaking part with Buffalo Wild Wings, I stumbled upon my next serving job.

To say it was different from B-Dubs is an understatement.

This restaurant was a privately owned Taproom. There isn't another one anywhere in the Twin Cities area. It was a massive, five million-dollar-a-year revenue-generating monster of a restaurant.

However, that wasn't even my biggest culture shock.

I was soon thrust into the world of **hospitality**.

My general manager at the time (who still is as of the day I sit down to write this book) is the one who brought this to life.

I was expected to not only reach but exceed the standards set in place for us. It wasn't a suggestion; it was a necessity, and if I couldn't do that, well... there was the door.

I was expected to refill their drinks and serve them their food and positively impact someone's day. It was expected of me to show integrity and empathy; it was expected of us to go that extra mile for a table that seemed like they needed it.

It was a requirement as a server to be personable with our guests.

Of course, every table is different, and differentiating between which tables want to interact with you and which ones don't is a skill that comes with time.

However, it was simply a condition of our employment to work with honesty, show compassion, and give our guests an enjoyable experience.

The bar for a server was set incredibly high, but instead of crumbling under this pressure, I thrived.

I was able to show my personality. I was able to not just joke with my tables but create actual, real relationships with them.

Not only were there high standards set for personable connection, but there were rules and expectations set when it came to food service as well.

It was unacceptable to allow a table to sit with dirty dishes their entire meal. Likewise, it was unacceptable to allow a table to leave unhappy without doing everything possible to rectify the situation.

It was unacceptable not to put your customers first.

Every day at our pre-shift meeting, my manager would talk to us about **empathy** and **hospitality** and how they go hand in hand.

We would have discussions about what really makes a good restaurant, and surprisingly, more often than not, food was never even brought up in the conversation.

Community, relationships, hard work, and integrity were the core of this place. They still are.

I know the way I describe it, it seems to be a little much. I know it may not seem like it would be a 'fun' place to work. I know it may sound like management had their hands around our necks waiting for us to slip up on their long list of rules. But, that wasn't the case. While we were expected to do these things, our management team also understood we are human beings. We make mistakes. Sometimes, we get behind and are so busy we don't get a chance to use the bathroom, let alone pre-bus our entire party of twelve's dirty dishes.

The turnover rate for new hires was high because not every person who came looking for a serving job was ready for what was offered. However, the turnover rate for long-term employees was low. This is because once you stuck around long enough to see the benefits of serving through the lens of hospitality and the rewards that came with that mindset, you were hooked.

I grew as a server there more than I ever could have imagined. I invested six years of my life into the four walls of that building, and even though I have since parted ways, the skills, lessons, and memories I made there will always be tucked away in my heart. They are now who I am as a server.

During those six years, I made irreplaceable relationships with regulars that have seen me through some of the most difficult stages in my life.

I learned patience, communication, multi-tasking abilities, time management, quick thinking, and problem-solving skills. All while doing it with a smile on my face (even on the days smiling was the last thing I wanted to do).

Being a server is so much more than bringing food to a table. It's so much more than taking a table's order and dropping off their check.

I mean, you CAN be that kind of server, but why would you want to?

Restaurants are a unique, special kind of environment that brings people together from every walk of life, every background, race, gender, age, ethnicity, you name it. Under one roof, people come together to bond over the universal love of food and the desire for fellowship.

Restaurants are often a gathering place during special moments in people's lives.

Birthdays, holidays, engagements, anniversaries - even after funerals, people come together to be served and be in the company of others.

It's so easy as a server to fall into the mode that *"this is just a job. It's just a paycheck."*

It's so easy to forget that your customers are real people with real problems too. Sometimes I forget that the people walking in the door and sitting down at my table all carry with them issues and challenges I'll never know about.

I go out to eat often, and although I am extremely understanding of almost any type of service I get, I am left disappointed more often than not. I don't mean that in a judgmental way, but the number of times I get a server who knows what it means to be hospitable is extremely low.

I did end up going to the University of Minnesota - Twin Cities as a Psychology major. So as someone who has years of knowledge of how human beings think, this gives me an advantage as a server. Not in a manipulative way, of course, but at the end of the day, we all do this to pay our bills, and our tips are our lifelines.

So, with all of that being said, here I am, a server of nearly eight years to bring to you my 101 best tips, tricks, stories, and lessons I've learned in the hospitality industry.

I believe with all of my heart that servers can do better.

And you know what? The money will reflect that, **I guarantee it**

# Chapter 1: Does This Apron Make Me Look Fat?

## How Your Appearance Can Make or Break Your Reputation:

### *Intro:*

Picture this: you're planning to have dinner at a local restaurant to celebrate your anniversary. Beforehand, you get all dolled up: red lipstick on, grandma's pearls, and your husband's favorite perfume. This anniversary is different from all the others though. You had no idea how this year was going to look after your aggressive chemotherapy stole your anniversary last year. You weren't even sure you'd make it to see the next one, but here we are.

While you have to be extra cautious of germs due to your compromised immune system, this is an intimately special occasion for you and your husband, so you grab your hand sanitizer, take a deep breath and head out the door for the first outing in over a year.

You sit down at your table, and your server walks up. You can tell they don't care to be there simply by their first impression. Their shirt has food stains all over it, and they definitely are in need of a shower. Their hair has more grease in it than the deep fryers in the back. In addition, as he takes your order, you can see dirt under his fingernails.

See how just the simple act of not taking care of yourself can be so off-putting to a customer?

I'd be lying if I told you that as human beings, we don't make quick judgments of others based on their physical appearance. But, unfortunately, you have only a very small, limited amount of time to give a good first impression as a server.

Now, am I saying go the full distance and do your hair and makeup every single day? Absolutely not! I know that for some people, either they don't enjoy wearing makeup, or they have lives that are far too busy to be able to pull that off before work every day.

However, I am saying that taking care of your physical image is important. You are handling people's food. Not their paperwork. You are handling things that are going to go directly into their mouths.

This brings me to:

### *TIP #1: You are Always on a Stage. Personal Hygiene is Necessary!*

When customers are seated at their tables, they are at eye level with everything going on around them. When people wait for their food, they often gaze at the environment, the atmosphere, and the people around them. This means they're probably looking at you too. So be conscious of touching your face or your hair.

The simple act of showering, brushing your teeth, combing back your hair, and making sure your clothes are clean is truly all you need to do to at least start making yourself look put together. Deodorant is your friend; use it!

### *TIP #2: Hide Your Hangover!*

In the restaurant industry, we oddly thrive off closing down at midnight, going to the neighborhood bar, drinking an ungodly amount of alcohol, and coming back in to open the next day. In terms of industries with the highest rates of alcohol consumption, the restaurant industry comes in third place only behind miners and construction workers.

Besides the long hours, stressful dinner rushes, "hangry" customers, and physical work it takes to be a server, my best guess for the reasoning behind this alarming statistic is because many times we get off at odd hours of the night when the rest of the world is sound asleep in bed. Nothing else is open, so what do we do? We drink.

Going out to the bars after work is just part of the culture of the restaurant industry. We all have a few rounds while we talk about our night. We complain about our coworkers who were promoted unfairly; we bond over customers that were upset that what they ordered "wasn't what they ordered," and we b*tch about the hosts triple seating us all night.

However, even though I know firsthand how difficult it can be, making sure your tables the next day have no idea that just three hours ago, you were sloshed out at Wild Bills is part of refining your craft.

Nobody wants a server who looks as if they might throw up all six of the tequila shots, they took the night before all over your table.

Take some ibuprofen, take a shower, brush your teeth so you can look good on the outside even if you feel like sh*t on the inside.

### *TIP #3: Make Sure the Cigarette Stench Comes Off.*

It's true that smell and taste go hand in hand. This is why many restaurants don't allow their employees to wear perfume or cologne.

The last thing any guest wants to taste is your Axe Dark Temptation body spray while they eat their chicken wild rice soup.

This goes for cigarette smells as well. An extremely high number of restaurant staff smoke due to the stressful work environment and ability to step out back after being in the weeds for 3 hours straight.

Again, servers, bartenders, and cooks have the highest rates of cigarette smokers behind construction workers and miners.

While smoking can undoubtedly give you a break, you need to get back in there and finish out your shift; neither your tables nor your coworkers want to smell that stench on you.

Before you ask your table if they'd like a caramel apple bread pudding, wash your hands and pop a mint.

***Tip #4: Wash Your Apron.***

If you were to walk up to any restaurant staff member and ask them when the last time they washed their apron was, I would bet money that 9 out of 10 of them would say never.

For whatever reason, washing your apron is something that immediately slips your mind the second you get home. Many times, servers keep personal items such as chapstick, wine keys, lighters, and other belongings in their aprons, so unloading it all to throw it in the wash is just more work than deemed necessary.

However, our aprons are the first place food gathers. When we bus our tables and have dishes stacked up, our aprons get the brunt of the stray sauce. When we accidentally get ketchup on our hands while running food, our aprons get the remnants of that too. Although, as a server, you may think, "*nobody is going to notice my apron is dirty,"* your customer, who's sitting dang near eye level with it, might beg to differ.

### *Tip #5: Dirty Fingernails are One of the First Things a Customer will Notice.*

Our dirty server hands touch *every single surface* in the restaurant. Our nails are front and center when we hold our book to take our table's order. When we bring beers or diet Pepsis to our table, our nails are on full display. This means whether you have a freshly polished full set or you have nails that look like you just fixed the engine on your car, everyone can see them.

It's a small but important detail in making sure you look polished and neat.

### *Tip #6: Take Pride in Your Look.*

It's true that if you act confident in yourself, others will, in turn (either consciously or subconsciously) feel as though you deserve respect.

This doesn't have anything to do with "pretty privilege" but rather dressing and appearing like the successful server you want to portray. By taking pride in how you present yourself, you're telling your tables they can trust you with their food, making them feel more at ease.

When tables feel more at ease with you, they unknowingly like you more. Liking you more leads to more generous tips. Catch my drift?

Their food is coming out of a place they can't see, being prepared by hands they can't see. YOU are their connection to the kitchen. YOU are the one ensuring that the food they're going to put into their mouths is safe and prepared in a clean environment.

All of this stems back to your appearance. It's simply the first and frequently the only thing your tables will know about you. So making sure you look clean and put together is crucial.

***Tip #7: Watch Your Facial Expressions.***

I won't lie; this one was a challenge for me. I'm just an expressive person, and I've been told I wear my emotions on my sleeve. I don't mean to; it's just how I am.

However, you are **always** on a stage. Customers people watch while they wait for their food.

Rolling your eyes, raising your eyebrows, or looking angry after being stiffed on a tab are all facial expressions that can come on suddenly and with a vengeance.

Nonetheless, it's important to control them and wait until you're in the back to express your frustration. Keeping it professional even when things don't go in your favor is key. Customers don't need to witness you blow up over a 5% tip because, in all honesty, it just makes you look entitled - to put it simply.

Am I saying don't be upset over a 5% tip? Absolutely not! Especially if you know you gave them top-notch service. All I'm saying is rant about it in the back of the house instead of on the floor.

## Chapter Review

So, let's give this a quick recap, so we don't start off with an overwhelming amount of information:

- While waiting for their food, customers like to people watch. Remember, you are always on a stage.
- How you take care of yourself is not only important to customers - it's important for your tips, for your self-esteem, and for the way others subconsciously treat you.
- Whether intentional or not, looking like you have your sh*t together even if you feel the farthest thing from it is a simple but incredibly powerful way to create a sense of trust with your table.
- Keep in mind, you are the guest's connection to the kitchen. Look like it

# Chapter 2: "Hi! My name is ...."

## How Your Greeting Can Set the Tone for the Entire Experience:

Let's think about this for a second. Let's say you're planning to visit a friend's house. Maybe this is a friend you haven't seen for a while or a friend you're meeting in person for the first time. You head on your way over with high expectations of a memorable night spent in entertaining conversation as you enjoy your savory dinner and glass (or three) of a full, robust Pinot Noir. However, they greet you at the door with a blank face when you get there. They do say hi, but their tone is flat, monotone and they simply say "come in."

You probably wouldn't feel very welcome or even wanted there. Instead, you might immediately want to go home or find a different friend to visit. Suddenly, the hope and excitement you had of a good experience has been diminished.

In a way, this is how important making the first initial contact with your table is. After that, they've entered **your** home, and it is **your** job to make them feel accepted and taken care of.

In fact, studies have shown people, on average only need seven seconds to make a judgment call during a first impression.

The first time you communicate with your table is your one and only chance to show them right off the bat who you really are. This first initial interaction can truly set the stage for how the entire rest of the experience will be perceived on their end.

### *Tip #8: Always State Your Name When Greeting a Table.*

This tip is even more important if you work at a restaurant that doesn't use name tags. Automatically identifying yourself with your name makes you more friendly and personable. In some cases, it can even spark up a conversation, making an easy entrance into small talk. If your table has someone present with that name or "has a granddaughter named Emma," this can create an instant connection.

This can then lead to a positive initial interaction. People are automatically drawn to familiarity. So, if you and a girl at your table have the same name, they subconsciously already like you more. This can easily increase your tips.

Acting personable and not like a robot is one of the biggest differences between service and hospitality. However, the simple act of just stating your name can go farther than you realize.

### *Tip #9: SMILE When You Greet a Table.*

This may sound harsh, but your tables are there to have a good time. They aren't there to feel like a burden to you. You have no idea if they just came from a funeral, from a difficult hospital visit, or from an incredibly stressful court appearance.

Whatever the case may be, smiling while making initial contact with your tables tells them you feel positive about them, which puts them at ease.

People often watch you approach their table before they hear the words come out of your mouth. Visual messages register **far before** verbal messages do, so making sure you have a pleasant look on your face as you reach their table can set the tone for how they feel about you.

***Tip #10: NEVER Let Your Tables Feel Your Stress.***

Trust me when I say, I've been there before: Your party of ten just got sat, you have a family with hungry children waiting to order, you have an order to go to the kitchen, a table that ordered soda water and the only gun with soda water is across the entire restaurant, a coupon you need a manager to comp, (*WHERE ARE ALL THE MANAGERS WHEN YOU NEED THEM*?!) the rest of your six top's joiners just arrived, you have drinks at the bar waiting and - oh wait... The hosts just sat me AGAIN?!

As a server, we call this *"being in the weeds"* - the definition of this restaurant slang can be thought of as a server or bartender who is hopelessly behind. They have so many tasks that their usual degree of service often takes a toll.

Essentially, we are so busy, at our busiest we can possibly handle - that we feel as though we simply cannot catch up.

As a server of eight years, I don't find myself in the weeds too often anymore. I would say it would happen the most during years three to six when I was seasoned enough to handle bigger sections but still hadn't had my own rhythm of time management down to a craft yet.

However, no matter how busy you get, no matter how far in the weeds you are, never - and I mean never, let a table feel your anxiety.

This can be incredibly off-putting. However, since your usual level of service will probably take a toll, the least you can do is give them a positive experience when you're present with them.

They may have to wait a bit longer to order, they may sit with dirty dishes throughout their experience, and they may have to ask for things far in advance, but if you treat them as if they're your one and only table and not the straw that broke the camel's back, I can promise you, they won't mind as much that you completely forgot to get them the ranch dressing they asked for.

So, even if you're eight tables deep in the weeds, put on your server face and approach a table **calmly**, thank them for being patient and concentrate on them and *only them* until you walk away.

Acting stress-free even when you aren't is an art. Master it.

### *Tip #11: Greet a Table Within Two Minutes.*

While nobody likes a server that immediately bombards them the second they sit down, don't ever let a table sit for longer than two minutes.

I like to give people a little time to get settled in and situated - but server time is different from customer time. To them, two minutes without a server may feel like ten.

I am convinced this is why you may see a poor review on a restaurant stating it took them "30 minutes to get their drinks" - No, Karen, it probably wasn't actually 30 minutes; it was probably ten. It just felt like 30 because you have nothing else to do but sit and wait.

### *Tip #12: Suggest a Few Options.*

This seems to be one of the biggest differences between a robot server's greeting and a seasoned server who knows how to be hospitable.

Instead of simply walking up and saying, "Hi, what can I get you to drink?"

Offer a few suggestions or show them where the drink menus are. By saying, "Can I start you guys off with any of our tap beers or in-house cocktails?" You're giving them the option to potentially get a more expensive drink (increasing your tab) rather than their typical $5 Coors Light.

In addition, by doing so, you're proving to them that you are knowledgeable on the menu, making them more comfortable to ask you questions.

### *Tip #13: Make Sure to Offer Non-Alcoholic Drinks as Well.*

When greeting a table and initially offering drinks, make sure to throw in a few non-alcoholic choices as well. For example, suggesting a flavored lemonade or a Pepsi product can make those who aren't drinking more comfortable.

In addition, it can be a suggestive sell for guests who were going to just resort to ice water: thus increasing their check.

Oftentimes, especially if you work at a place that has a large emphasis on certain alcohols (such as a Taproom or a craft cocktail lounge), people may feel a bit insecure about simply ordering a Sprite or a water.

However, people don't drink for a variety of reasons - whether that be they're in recovery, they have a medical condition, or they simply don't enjoy it - it doesn't mean they shouldn't have the pleasure of going out with friends.

### ***Tip #14: If a Guest Seems Indecisive About What They Want, Offer to Grab Them Waters to Start While They Decide.***

Pressure ordering is a real thing. For whatever reason, people feel a certain amount of responsibility to order *something* just because the server is standing there. So oftentimes, they'll choose whatever they usually drink, even if that isn't what they wanted.

By offering your guests water to start while they decide, you're not only buying yourself some time to allow them to think; you alleviate the stress of feeling like they need to order something, *anything*.

More often than not, a guest will ask for water anyways, so by offering it, you're anticipating their needs and saving yourself a trip in the future.

### ***Tip #15: If You're Slammed and Can't Greet a Table in an Appropriate Amount of Time, Stop By and Let Them Know You'll Be with Them as Soon as You Can.***

You'd be amazed if I told you how well this works at diffusing an impatient customer. When people first arrive at a restaurant, they often don't know what they want yet, but they do want to know they're taken care of.

If you have pressing tasks that require your assistance immediately, do a quick table touch to let them know you acknowledge them, you see them, and that you'll be over as soon as you can.

This easily eliminates customers looking around aimlessly, wondering where their server is.

## Chapter Review

- Tell your tables your name
- Smile when you approach them - this will be registered first before any words come out of your mouth.
- Make suggestions rather than the bland, "What can I get you to drink?"
- Give your guests time to think; this can increase your check average by avoiding them pressure ordering a $4 bottle of bud light
- If you're slammed, and it's going to be longer than two minutes, stop over and let them know you'll be by as soon as you can.

# Chapter 3: The Dining Experience

## So... What Exactly *Does* Hospitality Mean?

Let me start by saying there is a **huge** difference between service and hospitality.

Service is when you provide a basic need or task for someone. You get the job done, but there is little to no memorable experience. Often, service is what you'll find in entry-level corporate restaurants. The servers there take your order, bring your food, and cash you out. You got what you came for, but will you ever remember that visit again? Chances are, no.

Hospitality, on the other hand, is personable. You get the job done **but** with a focus on interaction and connection. When you show hospitality, you make a genuine effort to make your guests feel welcomed.

Not only does hospitality open the door for incredible conversations, new relationships with your guests, and a memorable experience for all, it opens the door for you to make significantly more money.

Now, as a server in a restaurant, there are two ways you can show hospitality.

Hospitality when **serving food** and hospitality when **connecting with your tables**.

In terms of food service, showing hospitality means being attentive, prepared, and observant about your guest's needs.

In terms of connection, showing hospitality means being personable by showing kindness, empathy, and politeness to your tables.

Hospitality in Food Service:

***Tip #16: Go the Extra Mile.***

Exceeding the basic expectations of a customer is the best way to boost your income. This is done by really basic, small things.

Someone asks for a water? Ask if they want lemons.

Kids order kiddie cocktails? Throw some cherries in there.

If your table had ordered a giant pretzel and wanted to box it up and take it home, grab them a fresh to-go queso sauce to take home with them.

People appreciate the little things, and these little things can make your guests feel as though they are taken care of far beyond what they assumed you would do for them.

Subconsciously, guests feel more inclined to do something extra for you since you did something extra for them.

***Tip #17: Be Attentive and Think Ahead.***

In the service industry, we call this "anticipating your guests' needs."

By anticipating your guests' needs, you're being a proactive server. Instead of waiting around to see if they need you, you take the initiative to prevent a problem from arising in the first place.

**For Example:**

A guest orders a burger with no bun. Then, as a side, they order a salad. As the wise server you are, you know that the side salad comes with croutons - so whether this is a low-carb thing or a gluten thing, bread and croutons often go hand in hand. So instead of waiting for the salad to come out and having your guest flag you down, you ask while they order if they'd still like the croutons on their salad. This prevents the problem from happening altogether.

By being observant of your guest's experience, you can anticipate any future problems that may arise - big or small.

Staying alert and attentive doesn't mean you have to stop and ask your table 20x throughout their meal if they need anything (actually, please don't do this). Still, by simply being conscientious of any future complications that may arise, you can show them you truly care about their experience.

***Tip #18: Time Management is Key.***

One of the biggest and most crucial aspects of being a server - well, being a *good* server, is learning time management.

As convenient as it would be to have four clones of you at all times, we aren't there as a society, yet.

Your goal as a server should be to learn time management *so well* that you're able to weave smaller tasks within bigger ones.

Of course, this is a skill that comes with time as long as you're conscious about it. Getting a feel for how long certain tasks take, which tables can sit for a little longer and which ones need to leave *asap* takes practice.

**For Example:**

You know that it's going to take you three minutes to ring in your party of 12's order because they all modified every item until it's no longer recognizable.

However, you also just got sat a table with parents and two young kids who most likely want to get the ball rolling right away. (With the occasional exception, most families with young kids almost always want to get in and get out).

In addition, your other table asked for a box and their check.

Which task do you do first?

Well, when you have strong time management skills, you know that you can drop off the box and their check, then head over to greet your table with the antsy kids and stressed-out parents.

This gives you a minute to allow your other table to get their card out. Then, as you turn around to get the kids their lemonades and the frazzled parents a much-needed alcoholic beverage, you can grab the check on the way out of your section and bring it back as you bring the family their drinks.

The family most likely wants a few minutes to think about food (because little Tommy "doesn't like grilled cheese anymore" even though that's all he's eaten for the last month straight), so this gives you time to ring in your party of 12.

See how you can weave smaller tasks within bigger ones to optimize your time?

***Tip #19: NEVER Guess on an Allergy.***

On a more serious note, there are hundreds of thousands of people who have life-threatening allergies. While this may make their outings riskier, it doesn't mean they shouldn't be able to enjoy a restaurant experience like anyone else.

As someone in the food service industry, understanding the crucial importance of an allergy is simply part of your job. But, unfortunately, it's not a part you can ever take lightly.

The last thing you want is for your table to be carried out in a stretcher because you were "pretty sure" the cheese curds didn't contain gluten in them.

Understand your restaurant's allergy protocol and if you *ever* have even the slightest twinge of doubt about a food item, always run to the back and double-check. (Don't ask the chef, though, he'll probably just tell you you're dumb).

***Tip #20: Treat Your Section Like One Big Table.***

This can relate back to the concept of time management, but as you go to perform a task for one table, make sure you're laying your eyes on all your other tables as well (in a casual way, of course).

The simple act of just walking through your section before you leave can save you five separate trips, which is obviously not efficient whatsoever.

People are often *fine* to wait as long as they know they're being taken care of.

Instead of your table sitting for five minutes with an empty beer glass not knowing when you'll be by again (because you're outside of your section running nine cards for your middle-aged ladies who "all wanted separate checks"), stop by his table on your way to the computer and ask if he'd like another one.

Then, before you cash out all nine of those tabs, ring in the beer first, so by the time you're done, the beer will be ready and waiting.

Even if it takes five minutes to run all those cards, at least he has the peace of mind knowing that his beer is on the way.

### *Tip #21: When Your Table Asks About a Food Item - BE HONEST!*

"The alfredo? Oh, it's really good! And the walleye, that's really good too!"

Customers can spot an untruthful server.

Being **honest** and transparent is the best way to win your guests' trust and confidence. However, you can balance being honest and selling an item in a professional way.

Let's say a guest asks you how the ribs are. You can say in a professional way that "despite them being a top seller menu item in the past, you've had multiple complaints lately about them being overcooked." This can reassure guests that you aren't just trying to sell them the highest ticketed item on the menu.

Also, how awkward would it be if you were to completely bald-faced lie in an attempt to upsell an expensive item, and it came out completely different than what you told them - yikes.

### *#Tip 22: Empathize with Your Guest's Complaints.*

"The customer is always right" I know, I know. I'm sick of that phrase too.

However, people usually just want to be heard. So, whether or not you feel like their complaint is legitimate, reassure them that their issue is valid and you're there to take care of them.

Even if the same lady that started complaining when she sat down, then complained about her appetizer, is now complaining about her entree, take heart knowing that often those people have much bigger issues going on in their lives than an "overcooked" well-done steak.

Unfortunately, servers and bartenders get the brunt of many strangers overflowing emotional baggage, and it's just part of the job.

### *Tip #23: Always Use Seat Numbers.*

Seat numbers are a concept used in virtually every restaurant to allow the servers to stay organized and guide food runners or other coworkers in knowing exactly who at the table ordered what item.

"Auctioning off food," as it's called, is the act of yelling out food items to a table and hoping someone claims it. It's tacky and can easily be avoided.

You also avoid the debilitating silence that occurs when suddenly, every person at the table has amnesia and can't remember what they ordered 20 minutes ago.

The first seat to the left is seat one. From there, it goes around in a clockwise direction to keep service flowing and coordinated.

As a server that has taken hundreds of bigger parties, it's 100% okay to tell your party you will start with your "first person" and work your way around. Yes, it breaks the rule of "ladies first"; however, it will save you a huge headache later when you're attempting to keep everyone organized.

### *Tip #24: If You Make a Mistake - Be Honest.*

Unless you're an award-winning actor, most people can see through a panicked server who forgot to ring food in and yet is standing there telling you the kitchen lost your ticket.

Nine times out of ten, guests appreciate the honesty when you own up to your mistake. We are all human, and we all make errors. Don't make up excuses; just find a solution.

### *Tip #25: "Two Bites or Two Minutes."*

This server rule has been around since the days when you'd have to write your order down and hand it directly to the kitchen (honestly, HOW did that even work?!).

Checking back after either your guests have taken two bites or it's been two minutes allows them the time to decide if their food needs anything to take it to where they want it to be. This could be anything from salt and pepper, hot sauce, more napkins, etc.

Not checking in with your tables shortly after they start eating means you could potentially miss a huge opportunity to allow the guests to not only like but LOVE their meal.

Happy guests = better tips.

## ***Tip #26: If You Drop a Tray - STAY CALM.***

In the nightmare event that you go to drop off food at your table and the tray jack becomes unbalanced, remember that every server who has ever existed has done this.

If you ask any veteran of the service industry out there to tell you a story about when they've dropped a tray, I can 100% guarantee you they'd have one ready for you.

For me, I dropped a tray on a baby once. Well, not a tray exactly, but an extra tall (20 oz.) lemonade. Right. On. The. Baby.

To make it worse, one of my managers - who wasn't particularly fond of me - was walking by at that exact moment.

No, the couple was not understanding. They moved tables and servers altogether, and we comped their entire meal.

But hey, you live, and you learn, right?

## ***Tip #27: Ring in Items IMMEDIATELY.***

This could be drinks, appetizers, or entrees. Whatever it is, if a table asks for it, ring it in as soon as physically possible.

Unless you've been doing this for years and years (heck, even if you have), ringing in food and drinks immediately greatly cuts down on the chance you forget to ring in a table's food altogether.

Let me tell you, there is no worse feeling in the world than the kitchen being slammed on a Friday night, and you begin to realize you rang in your table's food *a long time ago... wait... did you?*

As you make your way over to the computer to check, you begin to pray to every spiritual being you can think of that you did. However, as you click, all you see is a tab with 2 Mich. Golden Lights.

If you go back to the expo line to tell the cooks about the problem, you will quite literally get your head bitten clean off. So you decide this is the day you quit the industry altogether.

In order to save yourself the misery of informing your table their burgers are going to take an hour from the time they placed their order, ringing in their food as soon as you write it down will prevent that all together.

This is a lifesaver. Period.

### *Tip #28: Know the Menu.*

Know the menu, study the menu, love the menu. Having firsthand knowledge of each item will prevent you from having to run to the back to ask a question in the middle of taking an order.

In addition, this extensive knowledge will help with any guest's modifications, questions, allergies, or simply to avoid looking stupid.

In the event that a guest has never visited your establishment before unless you know the menu as you should, you'll come across as someone who has never visited your establishment before either.

### *Tip #29: Always Warn Guests About Hot Plates.*

If a plate is freshly taken out of the dishwasher and set under the warming lamps, it's undoubtedly going to be hot. However, your guests won't know this or sometimes may seem not to understand this (even if you're standing there as your fingertips melt off).

By informing your guests that the plate in front of them is hot, this can avoid the mess of any potential lawsuit (McDonald's coffee incident much)?

Being a hospitable server means not wanting your guests to get hurt. No matter how much you don't like them.

### *Tip #30: Never Set Anything Hot in Front of a Baby.*

Baby's are little grabbing machines. If there were a poisonous snake in front of them, they would try to reach for it. It's in their nature.

So, whether the plate is hot or the food on the plate is hot, don't ever put it in arms reach of those little suckers. Actually, don't set anything down in front of a baby, ever.

They WILL attempt a go at it.

If there isn't any place on the table far enough away, give it to the parents and inform them it's hot. They will appreciate the extra step you took in ensuring their baby doesn't get burned.

As a parent myself, this brings me to my first story.

### *Tip #31 (Storytime):*

When my daughter was only about eight months old, I went to dinner at a restaurant. Now, I won't publicly call out this restaurant but let's just say it starts with a "Ch-" and ends with "-ili's."

Everything was fine, and we were enjoying our appetizer and drinks until our server came out with a plate of steaming hot mashed potatoes. As I turned over to clear out a spot for our food, she set this plate down DIRECTLY in front of my infant. It didn't even register at first until I heard the piercing, blood-curdling scream coming from next to me.

I looked over, and my daughter had stuck her ENTIRE hand in the mashed potatoes. I mean, they look soft and squishy; I can't blame her.

I looked at my boyfriend at the time, then back at my server, then back at my boyfriend. I didn't know what to do. I ran to the bathroom and ran her little chubby fingers under cold water.

I distinctly remember an older lady following me in and checking on us to see if she was okay (bless her).

I honestly can't even remember what happened after that. I know I didn't curse out the server even though I felt like it.

However, looking back now that I'm a server, it's hard to comprehend why she would ever set something that is quite literally steaming in front of her.

### *Tip #32: Ask About Last-Minute Items.*

When you initially drop off your table's food, always ask if there is anything else you can get for them. Also, take note of their beverages; if they're under halfway full, ask if they'd like another right away.

Not only does this show hospitality, but oftentimes people forget to order things like ranch or extra ketchup when you take their order.

This is also a way to be a proactive server, asking them if they need anything to prevent them from having to flag you down across the restaurant for their 7th Diet Mountain Dew (true story).

### *Tip #33: "So, What's Good Here?"*

Even as a seasoned server, this can sometimes be my least favorite question.

For whatever reason, as soon as someone asks me what items are popular or what I personally would recommend, my mind goes blank, and I suddenly cannot remember a single thing on our menu.

Having a few items across different categories can help answer this question for guests.

Simply saying, "everything!" is not only a lie but unhelpful.

I usually will recommend two burgers, a flatbread, a salad, and some smaller appetizers just to give people a broader range of options depending on what mood they're feeling.

### *Tip #34: If You Don't Know the Answer to a Question About the Menu, Go Ask.*

I know it's a bit more work, but standing there in front of your table trying to guess the answer to a question is just awkward. Not only that, but if you're wrong and the food that comes out is not what you described, the guest is either going to be unhappy or make you take it back.

Either way, it all comes down to just being proactive.

### *Tip #35: If the Bar is Backed Up, Offer an Appetizer While They Wait.*

The act of simply letting your guests in on the situation at hand can greatly ease any impatience they may be feeling.

If it's the end of happy hour and every server and their mother has rung in the last round for their tables, it's no surprise the bar may be quite a bit crazier than normal.

In the event your table has sat for more than a few minutes, and their beers are still halfway down the ticket line, getting them water and offering an appetizer works wonders.

This trick is especially helpful if there is a wait to get in. People are hungry and have already waited 30 minutes!

Often, restaurants either post their menu at the front or have it online, so people on the waitlist will often look it over, so they're ready when they get sat.

***Tip #36: Pre-Bus!***

The art of pre-bussing your tables means you clear all of your table's dirty dishes other than their glasses off their table before they leave.

Ideally, you should clear each course before you bring out another. There isn't any reason why a table should be sitting with their leftover appetizer plates on their table as they eat dessert.

By pre-bussing your tables, you're creating a clean and more organized atmosphere for your guests and the tables surrounding them. In addition, pre-bussing your tables cuts down on the time it takes you to clear it and flip it for the next one after they leave, putting more money in your pocket.

I know that was a lot of information to throw at you, and I'm proud of you for sticking with me this far. It may seem like overwhelming information at first, but all of this will come naturally if you have the core of your service hospitality. Food service is just one portion, albeit an important portion nonetheless when it comes down to the very core of it.

- People come to a restaurant to eat and enjoy what they're eating.
- As their server, it is your job to ensure their dining experience is what they hoped it would be.
- Happy guests = better tips.
- You can't control the kitchen or the bar, but you can control the surrounding factors.

## Hospitality In the Interactions:

### *Tip #37: The Golden Rule*

"Do unto others as you would want done to you."

As a server, you're in a unique position that many other people in different careers don't have. You come in contact with hundreds of strangers every shift. Some you may see again, but hundreds of people you won't.

Be kind. Always.

Show empathy, show patience, show respect. Unfortunately, the outside world often lacks these basic core values, but inside the walls of your restaurant, you don't have to.

Everyone is fighting a battle you know nothing about.

You may have a single lady who comes in in the middle of the dinner rush and sits at your table. You may instinctively want to groan and complain because one person is taking up your entire four top.

However, what you don't know is that she just left home to get out of the house after her abusive husband came home drunk again. She needed a place to go to clear her mind that wasn't anywhere near there.

By showing each and every table empathy, you quite literally could be the only person who showed them kindness all day.

### *Tip #38 (Storytime):*

Years ago, my younger sister and I worked at the same place.

I remember one night specifically; she had a middle-aged woman sitting in her section. She told my sister that she was on a first date and she was so excited.

She was dressed up in a red dress and a full face of makeup. She ordered a drink while she waited. However, five minutes turned into 15 minutes. Fifteen minutes turned into 45 minutes. Finally, after about an hour, she waved my sister down to tell her she was leaving because she got stood up.

You could see her defeated face as she asked my sister how much her tab was.

My sister went to the back, packed up a dessert to go, took it to her, and told her not to worry about it - she wanted to take care of it.

The lady stood up, and tears started coming from her eyes as she hugged her. She told my sister that this simple act of kindness was the nicest thing someone had done for her in a long, long time.

See how easy it is to show kindness? At the time, you may feel as though it's just a small gesture, but to some people, it can show them there are still good people left in the world.

### *Tip #39: Find a Way to Make a Connection.*

Making a connection with your table is the quickest and easiest way to not only make yourself more memorable but to form a relationship with your table.

A connection doesn't mean it has to be this intricate, long conversation. It can be as simple as if you see someone wearing a sweatshirt with your favorite team on it, strike up a conversation. If you're a female and you like your guest's earrings, tell her!

The simplest way to make a connection with your table is to ask them what brings them in. Yes, sometimes you'll get a boring, mundane answer, but sometimes this can lead to a more in-depth conversation.

If small talk scares you, let the guest take the lead. Relate to what you can, but don't lie or fake it - people can usually tell.

By making small talk with your table, you can find out information you would have never known - this can greatly impact the way you serve them.

If you find out they're just in for a bite to eat before a movie, you know they'll want somewhat quicker service. If they tell you they're here with a friend they haven't seen in ten years, you'll know to give them space and allow them to move at their own pace.

### *Tip #40 (Storytime):*

Two summers ago, my best friend was serving a table on our patio. She's always been great at small talk, and she simply asked her table what brought them in that evening.

I can tell you by the look on her face when she came inside, she was not expecting what she was about to hear.

They were having a family dinner for the first time in over a year. Their son had just come home from being deployed and specifically requested to come there.

This was because he had been watching our social media the entire time he was in Iraq and had been craving our food for months at that point.

By asking that simple question, my friend made their experience memorable. She bought them a few desserts; we gave them a discount, and our manager went over to talk to them and thank him for his service.

### *Tip #41: If You Can Tell Your Table Wants to Talk, Talk with Them.*

At the end of the day, we're all just human beings. We all need interaction and relationships.

Sometimes I'll work a lunch shift and have a table or two of just one older gentleman. Sitting and talking with these people, especially the older generation, can be so fascinating, and there's so much wisdom to be learned.

You may be the only person who has held a conversation with that person all day. Maybe they recently lost their wife, and they never had any kids. By treating that table - even if it's just one person - as a human being, you're showing kindness and empathy in the simple act of conversation.

In addition, conversing with your tables is how you build regulars. Regulars don't come back for the food alone. They come back because YOU'RE there.

***Tip #42: Treat Every Table as if They're a Good Friend.***

Now, do I mean this in a literal way? Not exactly. Of course, the way you act at work is not the same as the way you act when you're in a group of close friends.

However, serving your tables the way you'd want to serve your good friend or grandma is how you should serve every table.

Make sure you give each and every table the best version of yourself.

Greet them with a smile, make sure they have the right food and drinks, be polite and respectful, ask them about their plans afterward, take their dirty dishes out of their way, etc. You get it.

***Tip #43: Make Sure You have Total Focus When You're at Your Table.***

Nothing says, "I don't really care" than trying to have a conversation with someone who's distracted.

Whether this is your server or your friend, being distracted while interacting with someone else is not only rude, it's incredibly off-putting.

When you approach your table, have all eyes on them. Attempt to close off from the chaos around you. Don't be looking around at your other guests or your coworkers. Pure, undivided attention is a gift in a world where we are constantly bombarded with distractions. Use it.

I won't even lie; one of my favorite things to do is completely ignore a guest from a different table if they're trying to interrupt while I'm (clearly) busy at another one. I can't explain it; it's just one of those little wins.

### *Tip #44: Know Your Regulars by Name.*

Anyone who has been in the restaurant industry long enough will tell you regulars are a unique, fundamental part of the culture.

Regulars are the hidden gems that keep servers and bartenders from jumping off the ledge when quitting the industry altogether is far too tempting.

Regulars are there for you on your best days and on the days where all you want to do is vent.

They are there for you when you get married (or divorced).

They are there for you when your child is diagnosed with a chronic illness or when you become the server with the big pregnant belly. (All examples of my own life).

The unparalleled bond you share with your regulars is truly one of a kind. Not only do you form a unique relationship you probably wouldn't have had the opportunity to otherwise - you connect on a personal level far beyond your regular guests.

This all being said: know your regulars by name. Even if they aren't *your* specific regulars, in particular, creating the atmosphere of treating regulars like family is what keeps them coming back through the doors.

If they are indeed *your* regulars, ask about their families. Ask about their lives. Ask about their wife or son who just had a baby. Ask about their grandkids. I promise you, not only will regulars take care of you financially, a relationship will be formed that you will never, ever forget.

### *Tip #45 (Storytime):*

### Mark and Deb:

Since we are on the topic, I should tell a few stories to help fellow servers understand the absolute blessing that your regulars are.

The first time I served Mark and Deb was around four years ago. I specifically remember what table they sat at and who they were with. It was Mark, Deb, and their older daughter, who just so happened to be around my age.

As I served them, we began making conversation. It turns out, it was the first time they ever visited our establishment but was far, far from the last.

Throughout my six-year employment, they never stopped consistently coming in to visit. During that time, I had gotten married, had my second baby, divorced, moved back in with my parents, started college, moved into my own townhome, started a new relationship, ended up having a miscarriage, and eventually shared with them my dreams of quitting the industry to become a writer.

Through it all, every up and down, every twist and turn, every heartbreak, birthday, holiday, even a freaking pandemic, they were there.

Above the vanity in my bedroom is a gold Hallmark card. On the cover, it says: "This Is Just the Beginning."

Mark and Deb had sent that card, along with a $50 gift card to Target, over to our restaurant after I had told them I was FINALLY moving out of my parents after leaving my abusive ex-husband.

Inside was a handwritten message about how proud they were of me, as they watched me go from one of the most difficult curveballs life has ever thrown at me to getting back up and standing on my own two feet for myself and my kids.

I had only planned on being with my parents while I figured out my next move (a few months, tops.) It turns out a year had passed before I could financially and mentally move on and provide a home for my kids.

They knew this and had firsthand watched how hard I had worked to get to where I was. And because we had formed this special bond, they wanted to show me how proud they were of me.

In such a vulnerable, fragile time in my life - where I felt so lost and alone, my regulars were there. They were a constant reminder of why I fell in love with serving in the first place.

Even as I move on from the industry one day, my regulars will never fail to warm my heart and bring a smile to my face as I remember all the life events they walked me through - loving me no matter what.

**Mike and Kathy:**

The first time I had ever met Mike and Kathy was when my sister and I worked together. They had actually met her first, and within minutes they bonded.

Mike and Kathy are the kind of couple that you hope one day you turn into. The positive energy that surrounds them is truly unmatched.

By the second time they came in, my sister and I were invited to Christmas at their house.

Over about three years of serving them, Mike and Kathy never failed to show the most overflowing excitement when they'd come in, and I'd be working.

Have you ever met people in your life that you can just feel, in your gut, honestly care about you? Well, that was them.

Just like Mark and Deb, Mike and Kathy remained consistent through many, many of life's challenges. No matter what mood I was in or what difficult situations I was dealing with at the time, Mike and Kathy were there with a smile on their faces, ready to make me laugh and give me advice as if they were my adopted parents.

**Regulars Through a Pandemic:**

One of the last stories I want to share has to do with the concept that regulars truly keep the restaurant industry afloat.

If you live in the United States, you're well aware of the tremendous blow that the restaurant industry has taken since COVID.

From my personal experience, it went something like this:

- Word of COVID began to spread. Would restaurants shut down? No, there's no way that would happen.

- A HotSchedules message was sent out to our staff to keep the news on at 5:00 p.m. that night as the Minnesota Governor planned on making a speech to address the restaurant industry specifically.

- On the 5:00 p.m. news, we were told to close our doors the following day - indefinitely.

- Restaurants were shut down... until when?

Our restaurant lost A LOT of money, don't get me wrong, but, thankfully, we didn't go out of business, unlike many other businesses in the Twin Cities.

- Restaurants all over Minnesota began dropping like flies. One by one, they each couldn't survive the financial impact.

- Finally, we were allowed to reopen!

- Glove changes were required every time we ran food or drinks, face masks at all times, hand sanitizer at each station, timers set to go off every 60 minutes to keep a sanitation schedule.

- All tables must be kept six feet apart, to the inch.

- No more than four people at a table.

- Wait, now it's six people at a table.

- Okay, now it's no more than four unless they are family, then it can be six.

- Not allowed to push any tables together to make more room - **no exceptions.**

- Use of water pitchers was taken away.

- No longer allowed to reuse the same glass; each person needs a new glass every time.

- We run out of glasses constantly.

- Limited hours.

- Prices went up.

- Okay, now we can relax - slowly, each rule is loosened.

- No, wait, cases are going up again.

- "Don't worry, we won't make you shut down again, but your bar can't have any guests at it. Tables are fine, but your bartenders are out of luck."

- Just kidding, "You have two days to shut your doors or face a huge fine."

So, by the time this second shut down had taken place, the restaurant industry had been **through the wringer** - to say the least.

The second time around, the government gave us two days to prepare and wasn't planning on aiding any employees with extra on top of unemployment. The maximum I ever saw any of my fellow coworkers receive was around $450/week.

(For those who have worked in the industry, you know this is often made in 1-2 shifts; so, our income was just sliced in half).

I worked dinner the day before we had to close our doors for the second time. Never in my life had I seen so many regulars show up and show out for our staff.

I had regulars left and right coming up to me, handing me money and telling me how sorry they were that we had to go through this.

I had regulars call me over to their tables, tables I wasn't even serving, to help me financially as we all tried to figure out what we were going to do.

Throughout the first and second shut down, our restaurant, like many others, survived off sales from carry out.

Our regulars were unrelentingly there for us every step of the way. Our regulars truly kept our business afloat with not only their to-go orders but their donations to the staff as well.

Without our solid base of regulars, our restaurant would have suffered much more than it did.

Regulars are the backbone of the restaurant industry.

### *Tip #46: Take Every Single Request Modification Seriously, Even a Child's!*

While it may seem like a pain to sit at the computer for an extra three minutes making sure your table's turkey burger comes out with no cheese, no lettuce, no tomato, extra pickles, substitute a pretzel bun and add crispy onions; or that your couple's chicken bowls come out each specifically modified to the point you're not even sure it could be called a chicken bowl anymore. It's much more of a pain to have to fix it after the fact.

Taking those few minutes of extra time will save you loads of trips back to the kitchen to correct your mistakes.

This being said, take every modification seriously.

***Tip #47 (Storytime):***

I call this one the mac and cheese lesson.

I once had a table with a father and son. The son was around five years old, and the dad was ordering his food for him. When he ordered the boy's macaroni and cheese, he looked me dead in the eyes and told me to "*make sure the spoon is outside of the bowl, not inside... just trust me*".

I could tell the dad was truly not trying to be a burden; he simply knew the effects of what would happen if the said spoon was tucked under the noodles (usual protocol).

As a mom myself, I understood completely. My 3-year-old turns into a spawn from the dark trenches of hell if I accidentally give him his yellow spoon instead of his blue one.

When I watched the food runner - an extremely kind and relatively quiet teenage boy - run the macaroni to their table, I immediately tried to make it over as fast as possible.

As he set the food down, I could see the spoon was, in fact, in the bowl. (Despite my typed-out message in big red ink on the ticket).

As quickly as my eyes widened, I heard a wail come from the table. The cry was a mix of distress and anguish, and as I watched the food runner stand there uncomfortably, not understanding what was going on.

I could tell he had zero idea of what to do. The boy was having a complete meltdown.

I ran over, grabbed the spoon from the dad, and told him I would be right back with a new one. I calmly took the ticket from our food runner and showed him where I intentionally specified they place the spoon on the outside. He had worked there for years; he knew this; he just either didn't care or didn't read the ticket thoroughly.

It turns out the boy was on the autism spectrum and couldn't eat his food without having it precisely the way he wanted.

In the end, the situation was resolved and diffused quickly. The dad was more than understanding, and he stated he too, had worked in the restaurant industry back in his day, so no harm, no foul.

We both made light of the situation because in reality, watching an 18-year-old boy, who has no experience with children, stand there in complete confusion as this little kid's world comes crashing down was pretty comical but, it became a great lesson to always read the tickets carefully and take every request seriously. No matter what.

### *Tip #48: Be Visible to Your Guests.*

Nothing is more irritating than a server who acts like they're Harry Houdini and wants to perform a disappearing act on you.

Listen, I came here for dinner, not dinner and a magic show.

If you're completely slammed on a Saturday night, I understand; however, making sure you're still regularly checking in with your guests and walking through your section is simply a part of being a good server.

Chances are, if your guests have the confidence that you'll be around again soon, they are less likely to flag you down or demand things from you immediately. Frequently when guests seem needy, it's because they fear they have to catch you right then and there; otherwise, you'll be gone again.

Make sure you stay in your section as often as possible to ensure you don't have guests wondering if they will be taken care of.

### *Tip #49: Don't Transfer a Table Once They've Ordered Food.*

It's a little difficult to explain this one if you've never served before. Let me try.

The dinner rush is winding down, and the thoughts of getting cut start to creep in. But, instead of thinking about the money you're going to make tonight, you start to think about how many vodkas sodas you're going to slam down across the street when you're done, which you hope is soon.

Right when you think it's prime time for the manager to cut you, you get sat a party of six. Your heart sinks a bit, even though you know you can use the money.

You greet them with your usual friendly, warm smile as they order a few cocktails and water along with them.

You get their order for drinks rang in (immediately - as a good server does), and as you're filling their waters up, the host informs you that you've been cut. (Why they always insist on seating you right before you get cut truly is life's age-old question).

So. Do you transfer them to another server so you can get your side work done, silverware rolled, and section swept in a timely fashion? Or, do you keep them and make just a *bit more* money before you go?

The rule at my job was that we weren't allowed to transfer any tables after they had ordered food. This was primarily because transferring tables from one server to another most definitely can put a damper on a guest's experience.

Once the guest has ordered food, they are settled in and comfortable knowing they're in the middle of their experience. By transferring a table over halfway through, you're telling them you don't and never did care about their experience; even if it's true, you don't ever want someone to feel that way.

If you're going to transfer a table, do it in the very early stages before they've had the chance to build and form a bond of trust with you.

### *Tip #50: Laugh - Even if the Joke isn't Funny.*

Have you ever attempted to crack a joke, and no one laughed? Yeah, it's awkward as heck and uncomfortable, to say the least.

Laughter creates endorphins - endorphins are those little neurotransmitters that bond two people together.

When you laugh with your table at a joke they make, subconsciously, you're telling them that you find their presence enjoyable, and in turn, they like you more.

We all like people who like us. So, if we know someone finds us funny, we're more inclined to develop a liking for them. It's just basic human psychology.

## Chapter Review

Listen, I know I covered A LOT in this last chapter. But, really, when it comes down to serving your tables with hospitality, follow these general rules:

- Genuinely CARE about your guests' experience.
- Be willing to go the extra mile for your tables.
- Treat every single person who walks in the door with kindness and empathy.
- Pay attention, be aware and be available.
- Serve others the way you would want to be served.

The core of hospitality is integrity or the way you act when nobody is watching. Going the extra mile for a table only benefits YOU (unless you work somewhere that pools tips, which I would advise you NOT do).

# Chapter 4: I Hate to See You Go, But I Love to Watch You Leave.

## How Making a Good Final Impression is Key

The end of the dining experience is just as important as the beginning.

The end is when you bring them that beloved white slip of paper with the tip line nice and bolded, waiting for them.

Throughout their dining experience, conversations could've been had, and situations could have occurred that made them forget how great you were at the beginning. But unfortunately, some people only remember the bad things.

This is why finishing strong is important.

As you finish off your tables, you're giving them one last impression of you. This could be a cherry on top of impeccable service, or this could mean thanking them for being *so* patient when you were stuck in the weeds for half their visit.

### *Tip #51: Never Ask If Someone Wants Change, Ever.*

The debate over this topic is quite the controversy. Some people find it incredibly rude when servers ask them if they want change.

Some people don't even listen when the server is talking, so they don't care either way.

For others, they may feel as though the server is trying to "trick" them into tipping more.

While this most likely is not the case, you greatly increase your chances of them taking that change home with them when you ask if they want it back.

The whole concept of tipping, in general, is sadly a heated topic of discussion that can bring out a wide range of opinions (99% of the time done by those who have never waited tables a day in their life) that are simply not worth the energy to argue about.

Never **assume** your table is going to leave you their change. After all, it is *their* money, and they aren't required by law to tip you.

No matter if it's $10 or 10 cents, bring them back their change unless they directly specify not to.

*Pro-tip: Instead of asking them if they'd like their change back, telling them "I'll be right back with your change" can often lead to them clarifying what they'd like you to do. If they want you to keep it, nine times out of ten, they'll tell you after you state this phrase - unless they aren't listening or paying attention, which is entirely possible.

***Tip #52: Pre-Bus.***

Ideally, by the end of their meal, a table should have no more than glasses on it.

Think about it; you wouldn't want to eat dessert at your own home by sitting down at a dirty table full of dishes with half-eaten food and sauce-filled napkins, would you?

While this can get tricky to get every single item, taking the big plates and dirty napkins out of the way is a great way to finish off strong. Being conscientious by bussing the table provides the guests and other customers with a clean atmosphere.

Your guests can relax after a big meal when your table is fully bussed. This can give them the idea of ordering an after-dinner cocktail or even dessert, racking up those tabs even higher.

There aren't many rules as to the process of pre-bussing. I mean, you're taking dirty dishes off of a table, simple, right? Yes, however...

### *Tip #53: NEVER Hold or Grab Glasses by the Rim!*

Sometimes, you'll feel as though a rule is a no-brainer in the restaurant industry, but then people surprise you.

When you're holding any glasses (or virtually anything that goes directly into someone's mouth), never, ever hold it by the rim.

Firstly, covid - ever heard of it?

Secondly, you're always on a stage, as I've stated before.

Many servers and bartenders, if trained properly, won't hold any glass from the top third up out of pure instinct. So, this really just comes down to a matter of hygiene.

Our dirty server hands touch every single surface in the restaurant; nobody wants to be reminded of this when drinking their seventh unsweetened ice tea.

Especially in the day and age of post- (or maybe mid-) pandemic, ensuring your guests their safety and your cleanliness are top priorities will keep them coming back.

### *Tip #54: Finish Strong.*

Trust me; I get it. You're on a twelve-hour double; it's been nonstop since you opened. You've waited on three middle school boys' baseball teams, and certain coworkers have voices that drive you up the wall.

You've been cut, but you still have a few tables left. All you want to do is collapse in the back and cry in the walk-in cooler.

Finish them strong. Don't just slack off because you know you're going to be done soon. Your last few tables deserve the same good service as your first few.

This circles back to the idea of empathy; you never know what someone is going through (I will say that probably 100 more times in this book).

Whatever the case, finish off every table with the same level of service. You may be tired, but sitting down with a nice, cold beer after a double, counting your stacks of cash will make you feel a lot better.

### *Tip #55: Don't Watch Your Guests Fill Out Their Credit Card Slips.*

So, I never thought this would be something I would need to address; however, I recently went out to eat with my daughter at a corporate restaurant a few months back.

The server was brand new (she told us right when she greeted our table), so I wasn't expecting much. I was new at one point too. I don't judge. I *know* what it's like to work somewhere with lax rules and no sense of accountability for how well you do your job. I get it.

I could tell she was struggling a bit, so I like to give her the benefit of the doubt even now.

When our tab came, I went to sign it, and she just stayed. And watched. I was planning on tipping her over 20% anyways (because I'm a sucker, and you could honestly spill an entire tray of food on me, and I would apologize for being in your way), but it was such an odd experience.

She didn't say anything. She just stood and watched as I filled out the little black lines and handed it back to her.

This isn't something that happens often, but it does happen. Don't do it. It's just plain weird.

***Tip #56: Make Sure to Say Goodbye When Your Guests are Leaving.***

As you approach the table to give them either their change or their credit card slips back, make sure you make an effort to say goodbye.

Feel free to change it up as you see fit. If you connected with your table at some point and they told you they were headed to a movie after, incorporate that into your farewell.

Something simple along the lines of, "Thanks for stopping in, guys, enjoy your movie!" This lets the customer know you were listening and paying attention. In addition, it gives them the feeling of being special and unique to you.

When they get up to leave and walk out the door, it's always nice to throw in an extra goodbye or "drive safely!"

Your goodbye gives the guests a lasting impression of not only your service but the entire establishment as well. If you can understand the importance of this, it will keep them coming back, meaning more money in your pockets.

### *Tip #57: Change Up Your Goodbye When Cashing Out More Than One Table at a Time.*

Occasionally you'll run into a situation where more than one table wants to cash out at once.

This isn't anything to stress over but an excellent tidbit to remember is to try and switch up your goodbye's when handing them back their tab.

This is particularly important if your tables are within earshot of one another. Your tables can most likely hear you, so if you say the same exact thing to three tables in a row, they'll most likely get the impression it's just routine.

Even small things such as telling one table to enjoy their night while thanking another table for coming in can often be enough to keep things unique and different.

### *Tip #58: If Guests Leave Personal Items at Their Table and They Haven't Left the Building or Parking Lot Yet, Run After Them!*

I would say about half the people who ask for take-out boxes accidentally leave them on the table as they go. If the guest is still close enough, absolutely bring it over to them.

However, what if they left behind a wallet, phone, or credit card? If you see these things left on the table and your guests are just walking out the door or are on the way to their car, run after them. Or power walk. I guess you could skip too, but it may not be as efficient.

This simple act is powerful as it lets the customer know you genuinely care about them, leaving a positive lasting impression and thus, keeping them coming back. They will thank you!

## Chapter Review

- When it all comes down to it, we, as servers or bartenders, rely on customers to survive. We rely on customers to come in so we can pay our bills.
- Making sure you're giving guests a well-rounded experience from the beginning all the way to the very end is important to establish a positive relationship with the guest.
- As a server, it's your job to make sure you are truly taking care of your guests.
- Slacking off as soon as the food is on the table just shows your guests that all you see when you look at them are dollar signs. I know I said we rely on them for our bills, and we do - but this is a fine line to balance.

Let's say you have company over in your home; you don't just ignore them and run away when the party begins to wind down - do you? I mean, I hope not, because I doubt they would want to come back if you did.

# Chapter 5: "We Have Pepsi Products." "Okay, I'll Take a Captain and Diet Coke."

## How Drinks are Just as Important to the Restaurant Industry:

If you're anything like most people, immediately when you think of going out to dinner, you start thinking about what you're going to eat.

However, if you're like me - or a majority of other people, you may think even *more* about what you're going to drink.

*I'm not driving... Maybe I'll get the strongest cocktail on the menu.*

*I AM driving... I can have one cocktail before my meal.*

*I don't drink... I wonder if they have other options besides pop? Is it weird to go to a place focused on beer and not drink?*

Whether it's alcohol or not, serving drinks is just as important as serving food. In our day and age, consumers want more than just the basics. Sure, you're still going to get a heavy crowd of Diet Coke lifers, but offering more to guests who don't drink is a great way to create a positive experience.

However, when that magic liquid courage IS involved, knowing how to serve alcohol safely will ensure your guests aren't throwing up on table Twelve's kids or that they don't walk out the door and crash into three parked cop cars (true story).

### *Tip #59: If You Work in a Restaurant with a Patio, Always Bring Your Tables Water.*

Or, at least offer it. Chances are, if you have the time to offer it, you have the time right then and there to grab it. Guests have a funny way of asking for water while you're smack in the middle of the weeds.

By offering waters, you're anticipating your guests' needs, which, research has proven, automatically makes them like you more.

Offering them water while sitting out in the hot sun also subconsciously tells your guests you care about them and their comfort level.

Not only this, but by offering water to guests who are drinking alcohol, you decrease the chance of them going overboard - like warmer weather and hot sunshine make people drink more and make the effects of alcohol stronger (as the body is dehydrated).

### *Tip #60: NEVER Swap Out a Diet Soda for Regular If You Can't Remember What They Ordered.*

This could also be said for coffee. Never, ever swap out regular coffee if your table asked for decaf and you don't have any brewed.

While, as servers, we've probably all given a customer decaf when they've asked for regular, and we didn't want to brew an entirely new pot at 11 p.m - however, the reverse could have serious life-threatening effects.

By giving a guest regular instead of decaf, you risk the chance they have a heart condition or some other form of medical disorder that prevents them from being able to consume caffeinated beverages.

Do you really want to look in the EMT's eyes and tell them you're the reason Grandma Ethel had a heart attack during cousin Julie's 12th birthday dinner?

***Tip #61 (Storytime):***

On a more serious note, this really can be devastating to some people if they're given regular soda over diet.

As I've stated, I have an 8-year-old daughter. My daughter is diabetic, which unfortunately means she can't have regular soda (and yes, I give my kid diet pop sometimes because I'm a bad mom).

We were out one day for lunch, and I specifically asked our server for a Diet Sprite for my daughter. We had no idea at the time, but she had accidentally given her a regular Sprite instead.

Thankfully, I was able to see exactly when her blood sugar began to spike. But unfortunately, her blood was so oversaturated with sugar she stayed in numbers 4x greater than normal - for the ENTIRE day.

This affected how we ate dinner, how we had bedtime, and even affected our overnight sleep schedule. In addition, I had to get up every few hours to ensure her blood sugars didn't go dangerously low after all the insulin I gave her to counteract the Sprite.

So, if you ever can't remember - always go back and ask.

Had we not had the blood sugar monitor hooked up that day, or even had one in general, she could have gone into a diabetic coma. That much sugar without insulin is dangerous for people with diabetes and perhaps other conditions as well. Take the extra 20 seconds to go back and ask.

### *Tip #61: Always Refill Their Drinks, No Matter How Many They've Had.*

Trust me when I say it wasn't until I became a server that I developed a strong, passionate hatred towards ice tea.

Never in my life have I ever served an ice tea drinker fewer than three refills. Maybe it's because there's no sugar, so it's easier to drink more? I honestly don't know, but there is NO way iced tea is that good.

However, as a server, it is my job to make sure my tables have what they need and what they're paying for.

As annoying as it is, and as frustrating as it can be, especially when you're busy, it's just part of the job.

### *Tip #62: Know Your House Wines and Rail Liquors.*

Knowing what kind of rail liquors and house wines your establishment serves is honestly at the bare minimum of what you should know. Nevertheless, you'd be greatly surprised at how many people ask this question during just one shift.

House wine is just that - an inexpensive wine you'd probably drink at home because of how affordable it is.

Your establishment will have its own house wine - either reds or whites, and it's often unique to your particular restaurant. So, knowing what brand and type of house wine you carry is extremely important.

This lets your guests trust that you know even the bare minimum in liquor knowledge.

(Nothing hurts my feelings more than when a table says, "Just ask the bartender." No, sir, I am fully capable of answering your question).

Let me be clear: You WILL be asked at least once a shift what your rail alcohols are.

Know them, love them - even if you won't touch them with a ten-foot pole.

### *Tip #63: Ask the Parents About Kid's Refills.*

Kids are savages; they don't give a crap about rules. I can say this because I have two.

You could offer a toddler nearly anything, and they would most likely say yes. This is why when you see a kid's drink getting low (or empty because kids chug their drinks), ask the **parent** if they'd like them to have another.

Instead of assuming they can or asking the child, by asking the parent, you're acknowledging and respecting their rules for their children.

I didn't start doing this until a few years into serving. The number of times I've been thanked for asking the parents blew me away. But, unfortunately, more often than not, the parents will say no or ask for water instead.

Had I just assumed, I would have been breaking a boundary the parent had set, and that's never a good position to be in.

Not only does this respect the parent's wishes, but it also prevents a power struggle from happening. If I ask the child, and they say yes, and the parent immediately says no, you've just created unnecessary tension and potentially a meltdown. (How awkward would that be if you're the reason for a full-blown public tantrum).

### *Tip #64: Don't Garnish Fruit on Your Drinks with Your Bare Hands.*

We all like to think servers and bartenders wash or sanitize their hands as much as they should. Some do a pretty good job, but others could use some friendly reminders.

As I've stated before, our hands touch EVERYTHING from door handles, dirty plates, and that unknown dish pit sludge. Our hands see it all.

When I think about this tip, I think about those infamous commercials that advertise cleaning products.

You know what I'm talking about: the commercials that zoom in on a particular surface and show you just how much bacteria can live on your countertops or in your sink.

Now, think about all of the bacteria that live on the surface of our hands, whether you're a server or not. So, when you reach for a lime to give your table's mojito the perfect touch, use a pick instead. That's what they're there for.

### *Tip #65: Make Sure Your Fruit Looks Appetizing.*

When lemons, limes, or oranges sit for too long in the fruit tray, they can either become dried out or slimy.

This can happen if they aren't used quickly enough, they weren't placed in ice, or they simply aren't fresh anymore.

This tip all comes down to basic integrity and the golden rule. Would YOU want your drinks garnished with fruit that looks like leather?

For drinks like a vodka soda, fruit is essential to give it any flavor other than watered-down nail polish remover. Make sure your fruit looks edible; it's really that simple.

### *Tip #66: It's Okay to Cut Someone Off.*

One of the things I hate as a server, and I mean really, truly hate, is having to cut people off.

I love to have a good time. I probably like it too much, if I'm being honest. I am all for people going out and having fun. But, when Uncle Joe starts to have one too many and is cat-calling his server, falling out of his chair, or stumbling on the way to the bathroom, it's usually in your best interest to stop serving him.

People WILL challenge you. They will try to undermine you and your decision. This is why it's recommended to confide in either a manager or the bartender and let them know the situation beforehand. This will prevent them from going around your back and getting drinks at the bar; it keeps others aware in the event they get over the top upset. (A drunk person, upset? Never).

Have confidence in yourself and your decision. Don't let a 6'3" 285 lb man tell you that you're being "ridiculous" by refusing to serve him another drink.

As of right now, 43 states in the U.S have, in varying degrees, what are called **dram shop laws.**

A dram shop liability law simply means if a guest at your establishment is overserved, and they leave and cause destruction, injury, or death (most likely due to drunk driving), the blame goes directly onto the restaurant and the employee who served them.

I worked in Minnesota for most of my serving experience, and these laws are very real and very much enforced.

No table is worth losing your job over, no matter how hard they may try to fight back.

***Tip #67 (Storytime):***

This story is one I will never forget. It was a normal, busy Saturday night, and my friend Hannah had a table of two that had sat in her section in the bar.

They seemed normal at first; the man was a bit much, but Hannah just chalked that up to his outgoing personality.

They ordered drinks right off the bat, the woman ordering a cocktail and the man ordering a dragon's milk. Dragon's milk was a beer we carried that was quite high in alcohol percentage and dark; when I say dark, I mean black dark.

Throughout the course of their meal, the man had four dragon's milks. Hannah was getting a bit concerned because now he showed obvious signs of intoxication. He was becoming overly friendly and handsy with the woman, and his face was flushed.

Hannah did end up cutting him off, and after a brief heated discussion, they left.

Well, no more than an hour later, two police officers walked into our restaurant looking for her.

It turns out after this man had left, he proceeded to attempt to drive and crash into not one, not two, but three police cars. (How someone could get that unlucky is absolutely wild to me).

Hannah, being their server, was being questioned intently by the police for her role in this accident. Thankfully, nobody was hurt, but since she was the last one to serve him, it was going to come down on her.

I can't remember what happened in that situation. However, I believe the cops discovered he had been under the influence prior to entering our building, hence why four dragon's milks ended him in jail.

The point of the story is, don't ever let the fear of cutting someone off risk potentially losing your job.

## Chapter Review

- Restaurants are visited for more reasons than just the food. Drinks have increasingly grown in popularity and knowing how to serve them efficiently, respectfully, and safely will benefit you in more ways than one.
- Most jobs require servers to take a course on how to safely serve alcohol, but if you're like my coworkers and me, you probably showed up to it at 8 a.m., hungover.
- Overserving your tables is a risky game to play, and unless you're feeling particularly lucky, it's better to be safe than sorry.
- Be confident in your decision to cut someone off. Drunk people will sense weakness and take advantage of it if you aren't confident.

# Chapter 6: I Am Speed

'Speed of service' is a term used in the restaurant industry to describe how quickly it takes an establishment to serve its guests.

While every server is different, there is no room in the industry for servers with only one speed.

It takes time to be able to read the room and decipher how fast or slow you should be going, but practice makes perfect as long as you're intentional.

Not only that, but every table will be different. Some tables want to sit and enjoy their drinks and appetizers before even thinking about ordering food. But, then, there are some tables that know what they want to eat the second they sit down - and they'll make sure you're well aware.

Just like with many other aspects of serving, speed is a balancing act. Serving your tables too slowly and constantly making them wait can generate a negative effect. On the flip side, serving your tables too quickly can make them feel rushed or pressured to order.

### *Tip #68: Whatever You Do, Don't Be That Slow Server.*

We all know what I'm talking about. You go out to a restaurant, and the server takes at least ten minutes to even acknowledge you. Once you order drinks, those also take another ten minutes to be delivered. Finally, you're ready to order dinner, but your server is nowhere to be found, so you sit, hungry for fifteen minutes before he makes his way around again.

While some tables do enjoy a more relaxing, free-flowing experience, this by no measure means you have to *serve* them slowly. You can still deliver their drinks in an efficient amount of time, let them know you'll come around again if they have any questions, and check on their drink levels in the meantime.

As a server, we have no control over the speed of the kitchen or the bar (even though most guests think we do). However, as the face of the restaurant, guests will automatically pin the blame on you if their food is taking too long.

Stopping by to let your guests know the kitchen - or bar - is backed up and taking longer than expected can greatly affect how your guests perceive you and your speed of service.

***Tip #69 (Storytime):***

Remember the server I mentioned previously, the one who stood and watched me fill out the credit card slip? Same place, same visit:

The service was painstakingly slow. So slow to the point I actually watched three other tables around me get sat *****************while she was still working on getting our drinks, we had ordered fifteen minutes prior.

Since my daughter is diabetic, she wears an insulin pump. So, when we go out to eat, I have to dose her a little ahead of time so that by the time the food comes out, her insulin has already begun to work.

Since I know kitchen times vary, I always give it some wiggle room and have really gotten this down to an art.

Well, I had dosed her about fifteen minutes after we placed our orders. Her insulin typically takes around 30 minutes to kick in, giving us around a half hour. (45 minutes after ordering which, I thought, was more than enough time).

Our server had only stopped by once, so it would've been extremely helpful to know if the kitchen was either backed up or if something had happened to our order, but after an hour, we still had no food.

Because her insulin was now in her body working, with no food to balance it out, her blood sugar began to drop.

If you know anything about diabetes, low blood sugar can quickly turn into a seizure, which for her has happened a few times.

After over an hour of waiting, she started to tell me she was feeling dizzy and light-headed. Our server just so happened to walk by, and I told her my daughter was diabetic and needed sugar ASAP. After ten agonizing minutes of watching her enter orders into the POS system, I decided to ask someone else.

I found the next employee who walked by and told them I needed a lemonade STAT. I needed something with sugar, or my daughter could die. God bless that server because she immediately went to fill up a cup. My daughter was already halfway through her sugary drink when our server finally reappeared with a lemonade for her.

I understand things happen; I do. But, if it's been over an hour and your table still doesn't have their food, it's imperative for you as a server to communicate with your guests. Had I known then, I would have ordered her a lemonade *just in case,* and we wouldn't have had such a close emergency.

### *Tip #70: Allow Your Guests to Take the Lead.*

If you've already approached your table more than once to see if they were ready to order food, and they still don't know, allow them to take control. A trick I often use when I see tables fumbling around for their menus as I approach is to tell them that they can stack their menus together whenever they're ready, so I don't have to bother them constantly.

People pressure order. I see it done all the time. I try my best to allow them enough time, but conversations get carried away, and next thing you know, I'm standing at their table 30 minutes after they sat down, and they still haven't even looked at the menu.

When I allow people to stack their menus, I can almost visibly see a sigh of relief because they now know that they can order whenever *they* are ready, not me.

### *Tip #71: Read the Pace of Your Table.*

Each table will have a different pace, and as their server, it's ultimately up to you to read their minds (or so they think).

Usually, within the first few minutes, it's obvious if your table is in a rush to get in and out or if they want to make this experience last as long as possible.

One way to read your tables is to see how quickly they are ordering drinks. If your tables all order drinks immediately and then turn to their menus, they probably have somewhere to be or a time limit on how long they can stay.

On the contrary, if your table wants to browse the menu for a bit, sample a few beers, or chat with their friends about what drink to order, they probably have a more relaxed time frame and aren't in the biggest rush to get in and out.

That being said, often lunchtime is when people are quickest. Many times, people come in during their lunch breaks, so they typically eat - and leave.

Nighttime is more flexible, especially on weekends. People have just worked a 50-hour work week and want to unwind and let off some stress.

Don't force it. As I said, it takes time and practice, but eventually, you'll be able to pick up on the little cues your table will give (most often, not even intentionally).

Go with the flow. Even if you do force it as an attempt to get them in and out and more turnover, they'll most likely just sit with closed-out tabs for an hour after cashing them out.

***Tip #72: Move with the Speed of the Room.***

It's pretty safe to say that the speed of service changes from a Sunday morning during a football game to a Friday night dinner rush.

In order to be a successful server and teammate, you need to match the pace of the room. So when it's Saturday night and you have a line waiting out the door, the expo yelling "runner!" every five seconds, and a well full of drinks waiting to go out to tables, you better not be caught dead just walking.

If you don't match the pace and energy and have a sense of urgency when it's busy, you will drown—end of story.

## Chapter Review

- Customers want both speed and quality when dining out.
- Being able to still give professional and friendly service while avoiding making your tables wait excessive periods of time is the key to making better tips.

- Read the pace of the room and understand that if you don't match it, you will drown.
- Give your guests time and space while still being attentive.
- Waiting causes negative feelings to emerge, which is the last thing you want from your guests.
- There are certain aspects you can't control, such as the kitchen. However, keeping an open line of communication between you and your tables is crucial to maintaining a positive experience.

# Chapter 7: It Takes a Village

## How Teamwork is a Non-Negotiable in the Restaurant Industry

A restaurant is only as strong as its weakest link. It's a ripple effect. When one server begins to slack off, this creates more work for the rest of the team. Restaurants operate by dedicated teammates who are willing to help when their fellow coworkers need them. From delivery to food preparation to cooking, sending the food out, reaching the table, and cleaning up after they leave, the entire dining-out process is only possible with every link in the chain functioning properly.

### *Tip #73: Many Hands Make Light Work.*

The restaurant industry is unique in that it's one of the only industries that truly thrives based on the relationships between coworkers.

Each job is necessary for a restaurant to run well, from line cooks, dishwashers, expediters, servers, bartenders, bussers, food runners, and managers. Without even one of these jobs, the level and quality of service would be significantly hit.

Research has shown that when employees feel connected to their coworkers and feel as though they operate as part of a team, their morale is higher, and they're more willing to help when needed.

### *Tip #74: Being a Team Player Affects the Entire Restaurant.*

In order to explain this one, I'm going to break it down with an example.

There's a station loaded with glasses, ice, soda guns, straws, trays, and all the basic necessities for servers. Unfortunately, this station is the farthest away from the dish pit - where all the clean glasses are stored. It's also farthest away from the ice bins, making it harder to refill than other stations in the building.

Let's say there are five servers using this well in a given night, probably more, but since their sections are near this station, we'll say five consistently.

Now, let's say they're all busy. It's the middle of the dinner rush, and the glasses begin to slowly disappear. Because some servers don't have the spirit of teamwork in their souls, they decide someone else will re-stock them. They feel as though they're too busy to do it, and if they wait long enough, someone else will.

So, another server decides to walk away from their section and stock these glasses. Even though they are just as busy, the station needs glasses. Doing this alone takes over five minutes, and by the time they get back to their tables, one needs a box and their check, one needs to be pre-bussed, one has been waiting to order, and another needs a third refill on Diet Pepsi.

So, then this server is now behind. This server is behind enough that they can't run anyone else's food or drinks for the next fifteen minutes because they had to stop and stock glasses. Had they all done it as a team, it would've taken two minutes, tops.

See how one person slacking off can have a ripple effect on the rest of the restaurant? Being a team player means supporting your teammates, whether that's by running their food or stocking glasses - each act is a domino effect.

### *Tip #75: RUN!*

In the restaurant world, we call bringing food or drinks out to a table "running."

So, when you stop into the kitchen to grab a tray of food that's ready to go, we call this "running food." I'm assuming you can figure out what "running drinks" means.

So, run your teammates' food. Run their drinks. This is how a restaurant will function efficiently.

You keep the natural flow going when you step out of your section to run other servers' food and drinks.

If you take a minute to run theirs, this just frees up a minute of their time to help you run yours, and vice versa. So you scratch my back, I'll scratch yours.

Oftentimes it's as simple as running a drink to a table on your own way to run your own drinks. However, loading up a tray with drinks to bring as you drop yours off can significantly impact how smoothly a shift will go for everyone.

### *Tip #76: Stock When You Have Downtime.*

This goes back to the example I just gave. Not everyone's sections will be synched, and you could have a period of fifteen minutes where none of your tables need anything, while your coworker could have just been sat a twelve top along with two other tables because "they wanted to sit in a booth."

Stocking while you have free time is extremely beneficial to your teammates. When you stock, you're allowing them to have more free time in the near future, and in turn, they can stock when you're the next one in the weeds.

Nobody's time is more valuable than others. By not stocking, you're telling your teammates that you are better than them, that your tables mean more than their tables do. This is a big, fat lie.

### *Tip #77: Move in a Continuous Path.*

As a server and a teammate, you should always be moving in a path that includes your section and the key points of your restaurant.

For example: Move through your section and attempt to stop at the expo line and the bar well to see if any food or drinks need to be run.

By making sure you're hitting all of these key spots, you demonstrate what it means to be a successful teammate. Your section is important, don't get me wrong. But, preventing food from getting cold and drinks from getting warm is just as important.

### *Tip #78: Build Relationships.*

I know this sounds cliche but hear me out.

What other industry **thrives** off of the relationship between their employees?

While every company in every sector benefits from their employees liking one another, the level of companionship between coworkers can truly make or break a restaurant.

Not only do the bonds between coworkers improve morale, but they also reduce stress in an otherwise highly stressful environment.

Not everyone understands the struggles of the food industry. But, from the adrenaline-pumping dinner rushes, the 12-hour doubles, and the late-night crowds that bring in their own sets of problems, you have to experience it firsthand to relate—being able to vent and bond to others like you is an extremely underrated form of therapy (and probably the only kind of therapy) for servers and bartenders.

This bond translates onto the floor. If you're in the weeds and you're able to turn and just *look* at your coworker for them to jump into action and help, you'll have a restaurant that runs like a well-oiled machine.

### ***Tip #79: Don't Bite the Hand That Feeds You.***

In other words, don't sleep with your coworkers.

I know I just made a whole point about creating bonds and relationships, but there's a fine line.

Successfully dating someone you work with is simple; one of you will eventually have to quit.

(Kidding... Or am I?)

In my six years of employment, I wish I could say that I came out scot-free, but I am here to tell you that no man (or woman) is ever worth risking your job.

Of course, you hear the (cute?) love stories of the line cook who fell in love with the server and lived happily ever after. But, honestly - it's few and far between.

Having to deal with either embarrassment or heartbreak while at work is about as fun as it sounds. But, it takes away from your focus and, ultimately, your tips. When you have to see that person during your shifts, it's extremely difficult to stay in the zone and give your tables the kind of service that deserves a 20% or higher tip.

I know I sound harsh when I say this, but chances are, you won't fall in love. You won't marry your coworker.

In all honesty, they'll probably move on and go for the barely legal hostess who just freshly turned eighteen.

***Tip #80: Never Piss Off the Chef.***

Fun fact: According to Business Insider, chefs are among the top ten professions with the highest rates of psychopaths.

Now, am I judging *all* chefs? Absolutely not. Have I worked with enough chefs to understand that entirely staying out of their way is the best course of action? 100% yes.

Whether it's the toxic masculinity of running and operating an entire kitchen, the overconfidence that's displayed as arrogance, or just the fact they're probably hot, tired, and overworked, stay out of their way.

If you want the kitchen to prioritize you when you make a mistake or respond without sarcasm when you have to ask how many of your appetizers are gluten-free, only speak when spoken to.

*I want to add I'm not talking about line cooks. Line cooks are angels sent from heaven. Hearing, "oh muy bonita chica," when you woke up late and had five minutes to slap on some mascara can really make a girl's day.

### *Tip #81: Tip Out Correctly.*

In the service industry, at the end of every night, as we collect our money, we "tip out" a portion of our income to bartenders and support staff.

While every restaurant is different, support staff are often the expo, food runners, and bussers (occasionally hosts depending on where you work).

Take care of your bartenders and your support, even if you aren't particularly fond of them as a person. Unfortunately, when it comes to bartenders, they often have to continuously pause whatever task they're in the middle of to make a drink for your table so that *you* can make money.

In terms of bussers, they have one of the grossest, dirtiest jobs in the entire restaurant (besides dishwashers). They show up every day to spend hours upon hours scraping leftover food into the garbage in order to help turn your tables faster and put more cash in your pocket.

I can distinctly remember a few years back when our serving staff began to rely so heavily on our support we started slacking off. Not only this, a large portion of our staff either weren't trained properly in tipping out, or they simply felt $3 on a Saturday night would suffice. Either way, we weren't taking care of our teammates.

Our managers caught on pretty quickly and decided as a way to emphasize the privilege of having bussers and food runners on to help us. They would take away all of our support (besides an expo) for a whole weekend in order to teach us the importance of taking care of our support staff. They called this the *day of reckoning.*

Tip your teammates out well. Without them, you wouldn't be able to do your job.

***Tip #82: Don't Harass the Hosts.***

More likely than not, the hosts are high schoolers working their first job.

Don't get upset with them about getting sat or **not** getting sat. They're probably doing the best they can.

The number of times servers would come up and complain to the hosts about how they were seating got so excessive that one host ended up having a mental breakdown. So, the restaurant I worked at ended up making a rule that we weren't allowed to talk to them anymore.

While this is clearly an extreme example, it goes to show that these kids are probably fifteen- or sixteen-years old working because either their parents made them, or they want some extra money to buy a bottle of Smirnoff Raspberry.

Either way, don't harass them. If you have a problem with the way they're seating

(and honestly, sometimes a rotisserie chicken understands rotation better than some hosts) bring it up to management, like an adult.

There's always the chance they stick around and eventually get moved up to serving one day. So you'll be working alongside someone you made cry on more than one occasion, and they won't forget it.

### *Tip #83: Help the New People.*

No matter how long you've been working in the restaurant industry, we've all been there. We've all had to start somewhere. Being a newbie is never fun.

In between Buffalo Wild Wings and the Taproom, I worked at another corporate chain restaurant for a very short time. I worked there for just under two months, but one server, in particular, sticks out to me still to this day, eight years later.

I couldn't even tell you her name because she quickly became irrelevant to me, but from day one, she treated me and the other three servers I started with like absolute garbage.

I never understood why, and I still don't. However, I'm old enough to understand now; it never had to do with me. People like that only treat others badly as a reflection of the way they feel about themselves.

New people have it tough, especially coming into a restaurant where strong relationships are already in place.

Lend a hand, reach out and help them; it could mean more to them than you'll ever know.

### *Tip #84: If You See Something on The Floor - Pick It Up!*

All of our actions really are for the greater good in a restaurant.

This means helping out if you see a table spill, grabbing a broom if your coworker breaks a glass, stocking straws when they're empty at a station you're rarely using, or picking up a receipt paper that's been directly in the walkway for 15 minutes.

The way customers view the restaurant will directly correlate to how they view you as an employee. So, for example, if you see trash on the floor, take the extra three seconds to pick it up.

### *Tip #85: Treat Every Section as Your Own.*

If you've never worked in a restaurant before, each server is assigned a 'section' consisting of anywhere from four to eight tables (on average). So, naturally, these tables are all next to each other, and that's your plot of "real estate" for the night.

Of course, it depends on where you work and the layout of your restaurant, but typically your section can change from day to day, so it's not usually the same every shift.

As I've made incredibly clear by now, teamwork in the restaurant industry is not only beneficial but crucial. So, when it comes to sections, treat every section as your own.

No, I don't mean steal your fellow servers' tables (please don't do this), but what I mean is, if you have some free time, or you're on your way to the dish pit already, grab some dirty glasses off your coworker's table to bring back with you.

If you see a customer looking around like they need something, offer a helping hand. It's probably something as simple as needing a new set of silverware.

By constantly looking outside of your section and treating every section like your own, you're allowing more tables to flip, more to be sat, and more money in everyone's pockets. Not only this, but when you take a minute out of your time to help another server out, they, in turn, have time to help you out, creating a smooth workflow for everyone.

## Chapter Review

- The restaurant industry THRIVES on employee relationships.
- Create bonds with your teammates; you'll need it.
- Pick on someone your own size, aka: don't harass the teenage hosts.
- Don't date your coworkers - no matter how smoothly they can shake up a margarita.
- Being a team player means giving a helping hand, being aware of other sections, running your teammate's food and drinks, and taking care of your support staff.
- When you operate in a manner outside of just you, the entire work environment will run smoother.

# Chapter 8: Me, Myself and I

## Why Taking Care of Yourself as a Server is Essential:

There are many reasons why the emotional labor of serving is a substantial load to carry. For starters, keeping up the appearance of being happy, calm, and pleasant for sometimes upwards of ten hours at a time is mentally taxing for anyone, but when your income relies on it, it can get heavy.

This is particularly true on the days when you're going through a hard time, you just received bad news, or you're all around just having an off day.

For whatever reason - and I could be entirely alone on this - bad news always seems to come right before you have to start a shift.

I've found out my ex-husband was going to rehab for six months, *right before work.*

I've found out I was being cheated on, *right before work.*

I've found out I was going to miscarry my third baby, *right before work.*

I also found out my 5-year-old (at the time) had taken a pair of scissors to her head and chopped her entire bangs clean off, up to her hairline, *right before work.*

The point is that when you work at a job that requires you to put a fake smile on and **keep it on** for hours at a time, it can become depleting.

Throughout your shift (or shifts, if you're on a double), you hit many often unavoidable obstacles. From mistakes being made in the kitchen, a guest complaining their well-done steak was overdone or receiving a $10 tip on a $300 tab (true story from a coworker), wearing the mask that everything is wonderful can be tiresome, especially when you wear that mask for 40 hours a week/365 a year.

With the emotional, mental, and physical stress that serving can bring, it's imperative to be intentional about taking care of yourself.

***Tip #86: Drink Water.***

No, energy drinks aren't water. So, no matter how much you want to believe it, three Red Bulls a day aren't going to hydrate you and keep you running (running well at least).

With the constant movement of walking (running if you realized you sent in a turkey burger instead of a turkey wrap and it's about to be sent out), heavy lifting of food trays and glass racks, and nonstop talking for hours on end, you're going to get dehydrated. If you're on a patio, the sun isn't doing you any favors either.

Drinking water is the best advice I can give you. But unfortunately, for the first few years of serving, I didn't take this seriously, and I woke up every single morning with a headache.

I began taking a water bottle to work with me and, at minimum, would drink four or five of those bottles. As a result, I no longer woke up with headaches, and I could tell I was able to last much longer into my shifts without feeling like I needed a walker.

### *Tip #87: Invest in A Good Pair of Shoes.*

Not only is serving mentally taxing, but it's also incredibly physically demanding. The exhaustion that comes from being on your feet and running around for hours and hours, often into the late night, can make you wake up in the morning wondering if you've just aged 40 years while you slept.

Most restaurants didn't build their floors with the servers' legs and knees in mind. Oftentimes they aren't suitable whatsoever for a person to be walking fifteen miles a shift on them. However, it's just the reality.

So, invest in a quality, nonslip, supportive pair of shoes. I don't care how young you are. I'm twenty-seven and can no longer sit criss-cross applesauce because my knees have been through too many dinner rushes. Trust me; your entire body will thank you.

### *Tip #88: Smile - FOR YOURSELF!*

As a woman, we all know there is nothing more annoying than when a man tells you to smile. For whatever reason, as soon as I hear that phrase, I automatically want to smile even less - weird, right?

However, when we smile, our brains activate tiny, little molecules that relieve us of stress. Then, neurotransmitters such as endorphins, dopamine, and serotonin come into play, giving us a mood boost.

Research has shown that when we trigger the muscles in our face to smile, our brains automatically create more endorphins to give us greater feelings of happiness.

Lowered anxiety, a healthier immune system, pain relief, reduced blood pressure, and improvement in endurance all follow, even if it's a forced, fake smile.

So, smile! Not for the a**hole who told you to, but for yourself. Free endorphins to get through your shift!

### *Tip #89: Never Take a Management Position.*

I've worked in the industry long enough to know that taking a management position unless you specifically need it on your resume is never, ever a good idea.

Not only will you be doing three times the work, but you'll also be taking a hefty pay cut more often than not.

Sure, that generous hourly rate comes in handy on a slow Monday lunch, but when your fellow servers are counting their hundreds after a chaotic Saturday night, you'll see why this tip made it into this book.

I've had quite a few friends, some of my best friends, become managers, and I've never once heard them say it's worth it. So unless being in the industry is your career choice (and absolutely no disrespect to any lifers out there), keep grinding as a server.

### *Tip #90: Don't Let FOMO Stop You from Taking a Break.*

On a more serious note, the lifestyle of the restaurant industry can overtake and wear you down if you aren't careful. Not only are the days long, the shifts stressful, and the endless problem-solving exhausting, but the culture can also take a toll.

Sure, it's enjoyable to go out for drinks after work, but the never-ending cycle of work, alcohol, and sleep deprivation can begin to weigh you down if you don't take time for yourself.

Don't let the fear of missing out (FOMO) keep you from making sure your head stays above water.

I know how tempting it is to say yes when all your coworkers are asking you to go out after work. I know how enticing it is to want to let off steam after a long night, but it's a slippery slope that can cause your mental health to decline if you don't set boundaries for yourself.

As I've said before, at the end of the day, you're in the industry to make money. You can't make those well-deserved tips by pouring out of an empty cup. So allow yourself to be in tune with your body and take a step back if you begin to feel drained. Your customers and your wallet will thank you for it.

## Chapter Review

- In order to be the best server you can be, you have to take care of yourself.
- Keep yourself hydrated with good old-fashioned H2O.
- Invest in shoes that will support your feet, ankles, and legs, or your entire body will feel the consequences.
- Smile for the sake of yourself and nobody else.
- The grass isn't greener as a manager.
- Don't allow yourself to become drained to the point you're constantly on E. Show yourself love by allowing yourself to take a break.

# Chapter 9: Tips with Nowhere to Go

## Just a Few Words of Advice That Have Since Popped into My Head

With eight years of total experience under my belt, there are so many more stories, tips, and tricks I could share. As I sat down to write this book, I felt like I could put the last decade of my life out of my brain and onto paper. However, as I wrote, one thing led to another, and I found myself knees deep, halfway through, with a pen and paper by my side, writing everything I had forgotten.

***Tip #91: Always, Always Feel Out About a Table Before You Make Jokes.***

As someone who uses humor to cope with pretty much everything in my life, I always thought that other people had the same appreciation for a joke as I did.

However, after years of serving complete strangers on a daily basis, I've learned this is simply not true.

Some people have different temperaments, and that's okay. For example, some people love an outgoing, witty server, and some would rather be left alone.

Some people come in to eat with the intention of having an hour of uninterrupted silence.

Some people DO, in fact, appreciate humor, but maybe they had been fighting on the way over, or they had just come from putting their dog down at the vet.

Whatever the case, your tables aren't required to be personable back. Always feel out a table before making jokes. You can do this by viewing their body language as you approach, attempting to make some sort of small talk and observing their response or simply by allowing them to take the lead.

No matter the situation, keep it professional until you feel as though it's acceptable to avoid coming across as insensitive.

### *Tip #92: Never Let a Table Feel Like You're Annoyed with Them, Even If You Are.*

As I stated before, I'm someone who wears their emotions on their sleeve. So if I'm upset about something, you'll know. I don't mean to be this way; it's just how my face is constructed.

However, part of serving is putting on a show. It's wearing the mask of patience and kindness, even if you're on your fourth double in a row and you've thought about quitting the service industry seven times today already.

If someone is being rude and disrespectful, I'm not saying you need to be a doormat by any means. But it all stems back to empathy. You never know what someone is going through. At the end of the day, you're there to serve them.

The table you can't stand that has asked for salt and pepper, hot tea with lemon and honey, extra napkins, ice water (that they don't even touch), nine ranches, and six Mountain Dew refills for their 7-year-old pays your bills.

### *Tip #93: Campers Happen.*

In the industry, we have a name for customers who sit for hours after they're finished. I'm not talking about ones who finish up their drinks and talk for 15-20 minutes while their meal digests; I'm talking about the middle-aged women whose tabs were only $20 each, who sit there for four hours with closed out checks while we're on a wait during the dinner rush.

I get it; losing out on an entire table for your whole shift sucks. But, on a good night, that table could've turned at least four to five times.

But, campers happen. Use this as an opportunity to focus even more on your remaining tables and give them the best service you possibly can to make up for the one you lost.

With one of your tables down, it gives you more time to connect with the guests at your other ones while also being able to pre-bus in a more timely, professional manner.

Even if all you want is to walk up to them and ask if they'd like a tent and a sleeping bag since they've been camping so long, don't let it ruin your night. Campers happen, and unless you work at a magical restaurant with no rules, there's nothing you can do about it.

***Tip #94: Don't Take Getting Stiffed Personally.***

In general, getting stiffed (customers leave no tip) isn't a pleasant experience, but getting stiffed when you don't feel like you deserved it hurts. It hurts even more when you feel like you bonded and connected with your table.

However, the key to surviving a world where your income is based on others' judgments about you is never to take it personally.

In my almost ten years of restaurant experience, I can confidently say that it usually has more to do with *them* than you.

No, people aren't required to tip you, and I'm sure someone somewhere will point this out to me (spoiler alert: I'm aware).

However, it's not just customary here in the United States; it's respectful. So, despite your table's mixed views on whether or not servers should "be paid a livable wage," it doesn't change the fact that tipping is still the standard practice in a restaurant setting.

So, when you put hours of time and effort into making someone's experience the best it can be, only to have them leave you a big, fat zero, it takes a hit to your self-esteem.

If a table doesn't tip you without any explanation as to why just chalk it up as a loss and move on. The same mentality applies as with campers; unless you work at a magical restaurant with no rules, there's nothing you can do about it.

### ***Tip #95: Never Judge a Table Before It's Over.***

If you try to tell me you don't judge people, I'll tell you you're lying. We are humans; it's what we do.

We have subtle, subconscious bias's towards strangers we've never met. I took a Cultural Diversity class my freshman year of college, and our professor made sure to give us a firm wake-up call if any of us felt as though we had no judgments towards others.

Server instincts are real, though. Sometimes, you can just *tell* when a table isn't going to tip you, or at least tip you 20%. It's something I can't even explain, but it's truly like a sixth sense.

This being said, people will surprise you.

I've had some of the best tips from tables I didn't expect. I've also had some of the worst tips off of tables I thought were for sure going to take care of me. Never judge a table before it's over.

***Tip #96 (Storytime):***

I was at work, like any typical day. I believe it was a Wednesday night. When I arrived, I was told I would be taking a party of twenty, which took up all five tables in my section.

I don't mind taking larger parties at all, learning how to serve at a place like Buffalo Wild Wings that stays in business because of large sports teams coming in; I have a good grasp on how to handle them.

The party of twenty was expected to be there at three, so in my mind, I thought they should be done by six, and I could still get a rotation or two in before the rush was over.

However, that wasn't at all how the night played out.

At about 5:45, there were only eight people that had shown up. For whatever reason, our rush had come much earlier that evening and was starting to wind down (for a bit).

My whole section was taken up for eight people, and as much as I didn't want to sound like a complainer, it definitely put a damper on my mood.

I had convinced myself I was going to walk with $25, and the night was going to be a bust.

However, the eight people that did show up took care of me. In total, they all left me about $150, much, much more than what the 20% tip from their tab should've been.

So, I'm serious when I say don't judge a table right off the bat. I had no idea that they were going to do that, but people will surprise you when you least expect it.

### *Tip #97: Always Ask for Permission Before Clearing Dishes.*

Even if your guest is completely done with their Caesar salad, always ask permission before just walking up to grab it off their table. I know it seems as though it would be less rude than to interrupt their conversation, but I personally have had 80-year-old women slap my hand away when I try to clear their martini glass from them because it still had one drop left.

I wish I were kidding, but I'm not. Just always make sure to ask. It's polite.

### *Tip #98: Using 'Sir' and 'Ma'am' Goes a Long Way.*

This is particularly true with the older generation. It can be quite refreshing to hear proper terms of addressment being used in a world that is becoming less and less formal.

Simply using your manners when talking to your guests can give you a reputation of being respectful and polished.

### *Tip #99: Socialize with Everyone at Your Table.*

Let's say you're serving a double date, and there are four people in your booth. You seem to really enjoy talking to three of them, as they are clearly more outgoing and social, but as you're busy making jokes and laughing, you ignore the one person who feels they don't know where to butt in.

It can get awkward and make others feel left out, leaving a bad impression.

If you're going to socialize and connect with your table, make sure to include everyone. Obviously, that can be quite difficult if it's a big group. But, if it's just a handful, make sure to look around and still try and maintain occasional eye contact with the other guests as well so the conversation doesn't come off the wrong way.

### *Tip #100: Be Patient with Kids.*

This could just be coming from my background as a mother as well, but if you have children at your table, be patient with them.

Many children experience extreme shyness, and by ordering at a restaurant (or being forced to order for themselves), they're overcoming the fear of talking to others, little bits at a time.

Kids can often change their minds last second or ask for items you don't even carry. Play along, smile with them, recognize they're just a kid, as you were once. I promise you, parents will eat that right up and are much more likely to tip you better if you were attentive with their little ones.

One time, I went to the dollar store and grabbed a few packages of stickers for the kids at my table. It was a small gesture, but I saw a substantial increase in my tips by giving kids that extra bit of attention.

### *Tip #101: HAVE FUN!*

Okay, I know this is probably the most cliche way to end this book but hear me out.

Serving is fun. It's supposed to be fun, if you want it to be.

There truly is no type of rush like being in the weeds on a Saturday night, with your friends nearby, running around like a chicken with its head cut off. Then, at the end of a chaotic night, sitting down to count your 20's.

Yes, you're getting paid to take orders, clear off dirty dishes and sweep french fries out from under your tables, but you're also getting paid to simply connect with people.

No matter how long the doubles get, no matter how many times you hear "I NEED FOOD RUNNERS!", no matter how many nights you don't get off work until the bar closes, just know that (unless you're a lifer) this time will eventually come to an end.

Enjoy serving while you can. Enjoy the thrill of making $400 in a 6-hour dinner shift. Enjoy the pride you feel when your guests compliment your service. Enjoy the little things, like not having to work sitting down at a computer all day.

Serving doesn't have to be boring or repetitive. But it's all up to you to make that happen.

## Chapter Review

- Not every table will want to joke with you. There is nothing you can do about it. Make sure you always feel it out first. Sometimes, you'll get campers. Use this extra time to give your other tables the best service possible.
- Don't take getting stiffed on a check - personally, unless you really messed up - it's generally not because of you.
- Make sure to include everyone! Use your manners and be polite.
- Don't allow serving to stress you out too much - it's just food. Serving is fun if you allow it to be.

# So, What Now?

It's never, ever too late to become a better server. It's never too late to refine your craft, even if serving isn't in your 10-year plan.

Being a genuinely good server, all comes down to this: Take care of your guests in every way you can, period.

Make sure they feel welcomed. Make sure you give them enough time and space (but not *too* much... it's a balancing act!) to properly make decisions. Treat them the way you'd want to be treated. Go above and beyond. This doesn't have to be a grand gesture by any means, but even small acts can make a world of difference.

Living in a society that pushes the mantra of "making an impact on the world" before we die, working as "just a server" can sometimes feel like you aren't doing anything meaningful. So you serve food and drinks, big deal, right?

Wrong. I can tell you right here, right now, that serving has opened up so many doors of possibility to positively impact the lives of the guests at my tables. I have so many more stories I could share and so many memories I've made when I started to view serving as a way to genuinely connect with strangers. I can't even tell you the number of times I've ended up physically sitting down with my guests and having heart-to-heart discussions that I can promise you, I never imagined having as I walked into work that day.

I've bonded with other diabetic guests over my daughter's chronic illness to the point I've had a table I had never served before give me their phone number in the event I ever ran out of insulin or supplies.

Like I've said before:

The money will follow, I promise.

It's okay to initially feel like you just want to serve because of the income. Many people that start in this industry don't do it for the late nights and endless miles on their feet. They come into serving with the mindset that they want to make money. This is completely normal.

But, if you fall into the mindset that serving is just a job and nothing more, you'll be missing out on some of the most incredible moments in humanity.

# FAQ From The World Wide Web:

## • Is it rude to use the term 'waiter' or 'waitress'?

A: Think of the terms' waiter' and 'waitress' like 'actor' and 'actress.' They clearly have connotations to someone's gender identity. However, unlike 'actor' and 'actress,' there is a third, gender-neutral option, 'server.'

I wouldn't particularly say it's *rude* to call your server 'waiter' or 'waitress,' but as a millennial, I would say it's greatly outdated. As a society, we have come quite far over the last few years to open up the discussion surrounding gender identity.

Whether or not you agree or disagree about the topic, it really doesn't matter. It isn't hard to just be polite and use the term server. Even if you're strongly against gender-neutral terms, I can guarantee you, calling someone a 'waiter' or 'waitress' isn't going to do anything about the situation.

You aren't going to suddenly change someone's mind or feelings about gender identity simply because you call them the wrong pronoun. So, whenever you go out, just keep in mind what I've repeated over and over in this book: you never know what someone is going through. You have no clue what your server has to deal with in their personal lives. We can all agree life is tough. So don't be someone who goes out of their way to make it harder.

## • What do restaurants look for in a server?

One of the most important qualities employers look for in a server is trustworthiness. Servers handle the restaurant's transactions, credit cards, and cash, so ensuring you're hiring someone who won't steal from the company is of utmost importance.

In addition, since servers are the primary point of service for guests, employers do look for well-groomed, hygienic, outgoing, and enthusiastic people. As a hiring manager, you want to have confidence your guests are receiving top-notch service because, at the end of the day, you're trusting your employees to go out and make money for your company.

Lastly, one thing I'm extremely passionate about is charisma. I am a firm believer that all the technicalities of service that come along with serving can be taught.

You can teach someone to write an order down; you can teach someone where all the buttons are located in the computer; you can teach someone to run a credit card. All of that can be taught.

However, personality is an innate part of who that person is, down to their core. You can't teach someone to be outgoing, patient, or level-headed under pressure. You can't teach someone to have empathy or compassion. Those things are natural.

As the old restaurant saying goes, "You don't hire great servers; you hire great people."

### • What does the job of a server entail?

If you were to look this question up on Google, you'd see in big, bold letters: "The job of a server entails taking food orders from patrons and delivering their food to them." However, we in the hospitality community know that is just the tip of the iceberg.

Since I spent the majority of this book explaining what life is like as a server, I'll bring up some other examples.

As a server, you'll most likely have to problem-solve every single shift. This can vary from whether a guest doesn't like their food, the kitchen made it wrong, the bar is taking fifteen minutes to pour one beer, whatever the case may be. It's up to you to make it better for each and every guest at your tables.

In addition, you'll be checking guests' IDs for alcohol, running your teammates' food and drinks, keeping the server stations stocked, helping out at the host stand if they need it, brewing coffee or iced tea, rolling silverware, etc. I think you see where I'm going. There are so many little tasks within every shift that servers are continuously performing I could write an entire chapter just on that.

- **What skills do you need to be a server?**

In addition to reading and writing, what being a server really boils down to is whether or not you can manage your time well, communicate effectively, multitask, think ahead, and still find ways to connect with your tables. I know it may sound overwhelming at first, but all of this is happening at the same time.

As long as you find your rhythm, know your internal clock and keep a constant flow of your tables in your head at all times, you'll be ready to take on whatever dinner rush comes your way.

- **How do servers know which table is which?**

Every restaurant will vary slightly in how they make their floor charts. I've worked at restaurants where they used a whiteboard. I've worked at restaurants where they wrote it out on a piece of paper. I've also worked places where it was all on an iPad. Whatever the case may be, each table in the restaurant is given a different number. It's laid out on the floor chart and often has a specific layout to it in order to help the staff remember tables easier

For example, all the tables in the bar may be ordered from 50-58. All the tables out on the patio may be ordered 90-98. So, as the floor chart is made at the beginning of every shift, each server is assigned a specific block of tables to take care of for the night. These tables will always be next to each other in order to avoid running from one end of the restaurant to the other.

- **How do servers know when food is ready?**

As I've said previously, each restaurant will vary slightly in how they operate. With exceptions, as always, there is usually an expeditor, who will tray up the food as the kitchen prepares it. The expo may know the food is done when a ticket prints, a screen beeps, or simply by looking for it.

Once the food is trayed, a food runner will take the tray and bring it out. However, this isn't always the case, such as in restaurants where food runners don't exist, when food runners are working that day, or when there is too much food for one runner to handle. That's when you'll hear the lovely screech of "RUNNER!" from the line.

This means food is up and needs a server to run it. Every once in a while, you'll get lucky, and it will be your table's food, but more often than not, it's a teammate. It doesn't matter; run it.

- **What is a side work checklist?**

"Side work" for servers is the restaurant term meaning what other tasks outside of serving tables you have to complete in order to leave for the night. This usually includes tasks like washing glass mats, wiping down pop machines, soaking soda guns, stocking straws, running dirty trays through the dishwasher, and wiping down the surfaces within your specific sidework.

Essentially, sidework is a way to ensure the next shift coming in has everything they need. So for the day shift, this usually means stocking as much as possible. Night servers typically carry the brunt of the work as they're usually required to tear down and build backup server stations as they get cleaned and sanitized for the next day of business.

- **How much do servers make an hour?**

This is a question I often find people are shocked to learn the answer to. Of course, each state has its own rules and regulations, but a large portion of states in the U.S pay their servers anywhere from $2.13/hr - $3.00/hr.

While I know this seems illegal, the government put this "minimum tipped wage" law into effect to offset the number of money servers make from their credit card tips. In a nutshell, unlike the kitchen staff, servers are making tips from their tables. So, the government saw fit that restaurants only should be paying their servers, essentially pennies and dimes.

Even in states with a normal minimum wage in place, like Minnesota (where most of my experience happened), every credit card tip entered during your shift gets taxed. Those taxes get taken out of your paychecks. There have been many times I've worked two 40-hour weeks only to see a zero staring back at me as I opened my check.

- **How old do I need to be to become a server?**

The age of employment for a server all comes down to whatever state you're working in. The typical age for a server is between sixteen and eighteen. However, minors aren't allowed to touch any alcohol glasses, making it incredibly difficult if you work somewhere that serves beer and cocktails. For this reason, many times, restaurants won't hire servers under eighteen.

# About The Author

Emma Eliason has been working as a server for nearly a decade. Starting at 19 years old, she knew she needed to be able to provide a better life for herself and her daughter. Now, eight years later, she shares the wisdom and humor she has picked up along the way. Emma has a strong passion when it comes to servers understanding their endless potential to positively impact someone's day or even their life. With tips focused on empathy and hospitality, Emma shares how she's been able to financially support two kids on server income alone while taking pride in her skills as a seasoned veteran of the restaurant industry.

HowExpert publishes how to guides by everyday experts. Visit HowExpert.com to learn more.

# Recommended Resources

- HowExpert.com – Quick 'How To' Guides on All Topics from A to Z by Everyday Experts.
- HowExpert.com/free – Free HowExpert Email Newsletter.
- HowExpert.com/books – HowExpert Books
- HowExpert.com/courses – HowExpert Courses
- HowExpert.com/clothing – HowExpert Clothing
- HowExpert.com/membership – HowExpert Membership Site
- HowExpert.com/affiliates – HowExpert Affiliate Program
- HowExpert.com/jobs – HowExpert Jobs
- HowExpert.com/writers – Write About Your #1 Passion/Knowledge/Expertise & Become a HowExpert Author.
- HowExpert.com/resources – Additional HowExpert Recommended Resources
- YouTube.com/HowExpert – Subscribe to HowExpert YouTube.
- Instagram.com/HowExpert – Follow HowExpert on Instagram.
- Facebook.com/HowExpert – Follow HowExpert on Facebook.
- TikTok.com/@HowExpert – Follow HowExpert on TikTok.

Printed in Great Britain
by Amazon

10976601R00068